John Gregorson Campbell, Duncan MacIsaac, Jessie Wallace

Clan Traditions and Popular Tales of the Western Highlands and Islands

John Gregorson Campbell, Duncan MacIsaac, Jessie Wallace

Clan Traditions and Popular Tales of the Western Highlands and Islands

ISBN/EAN: 9783744693585

Printed in Europe, USA, Canada, Australia, Japan

Cover: Foto ©ninafisch / pixelio.de

More available books at **www.hansebooks.com**

WAIFS AND STRAYS OF CELTIC TRADITION.

ARGYLLSHIRE SERIES. — No. V.

CLAN TRADITIONS AND POPULAR TALES

OF THE

WESTERN HIGHLANDS AND ISLANDS,

Collected from Oral Sources

BY THE LATE

Rev. JOHN GREGORSON CAMPBELL,

MINISTER OF TIREE.

SELECTED FROM THE AUTHOR'S MS. REMAINS,

AND EDITED BY

JESSIE WALLACE AND DUNCAN MAC ISAAC,

WITH INTRODUCTION BY

ALFRED NUTT.

PORTRAIT OF THE AUTHOR AND ILLUSTRATIONS.

LONDON:

DAVID NUTT, 270-271 STRAND.

1895.

CONTENTS.

STORIES ABOUT THE FAIRIES.

FOLK TALES.

BEAST FABLES.

BOY'S GAMES

APPENDIX.

PREFACE.

It has been thought well and due, by those who knew the late J. G. Campbell of Tiree, to give to the public more tales collected by him, and his sister has made over the following collection, selected by herself from among the tales gathered in the course of many years. We send them forth as a fitting memorial to his memory, and as another stone added to the cairn lovingly erected by old friends. At the end will be found a few letters which passed between the late minister and the late Iain Campbell of Islay, showing the methods of collecting followed by these two lovers of the folk-lore of their native land, and which in consequence cannot but prove of interest and value to those who have followed the steps of the gleaning of folk-tales throughout the British Isles—we may add throughout the world. These patient labourers in such fields were the true pioneers of the movement in Scotland.

Notes, where not otherwise stated, are the author's or editors'; those signed A.N. are due to Mr. Alfred Nutt; those signed A.C. to the undersigned.

Archibald Campbell.

Feb. 11, 1895.

INTRODUCTION.

MEMOIR OF THE LATE JOHN GREGORSON CAMPBELL,

MINISTER OF TIREE.

[*The following Memoir is chiefly from information given by Mr.
Campbell's sister, Mrs. Wallace of Hynish, thanks to whose
unwearied and sympathetic assistance it was that the previous
volume in the series, 'The Fians,' was made ready for and
passed through the press, and that the present volume has
been selected and put together from the mass of the material
left by the author*].

JOHN GREGORSON CAMPBELL was born at Kingairloch, in
Argyllshire, in the year 1836, the second son and fourth child
of Captain Campbell of the *Cygnet* and of Helen MacGregor,
his wife. The fondness for study, the devotion to his native
literature and lore, which were such marked features of his life,
and which earned for him an abiding reputation as a Gaelic
student, would seem to have been his by birthright. His
maternal grandfather was an ardent Gael, as may be judged by
the letters that passed between him and Dr. Mackintosh. On
his mother's side he was descended from Duncan MacGregor,
13th in direct descent from the first MacGregor who settled at
Roro, in Glenlyon, Perthshire, whilst through a paternal
ancestor he traced back to a race that had had dealings with
the 'good people,' and on whom a *bean shith* had laid the spell
'they shall grow like the rush and wither like the fern' *(fàsaidh
iad mar an luachair 's crìonaidh iad mar an raineach).*

The house of his birth on the shores of Loch Linnhe was
small and lonely, and when he was three years of age his parents
removed to Appin. His childhood was that of many young

Highlanders. From earliest boyhood he attended the parish school in the Strath of Appin, walking daily with his older sisters the long stretch that separated it from his father's home. He loved to recall his early schooldays, and their memory was ever dear to him. He had learnt more, he was wont to say in after years, at that school than at all his other schools put together. And on the hillside and along the valley, traversed twice daily, he drank in a love for and knowledge of nature in all her manifestations that remained to him as a priceless possession throughout life. At ten he was sent to Glasgow for further schooling, passed first through the Andersonian University, and went thence to the High School, preparatory to entering College. We have interesting glimpses of him at this period. He seems to have been a dreamy, quick-witted but somewhat indolent lad of whom his masters said, 'if Campbell likes to work no one can beat him'; hot-tempered too, as Highlanders, rightly or wrongly, are credited with being. The only Highlander in the school, he had doubtless much to put up with. His Glasgow schoolfellows had probably as little liking for Highlanders as Baillie Nicol Jarvie himself, and many were the petty persecutions he had to endure. He has himself related how he suffered several hours imprisonment for fighting another boy 'on account of my country.' Like all who are steadily bilingual from early youth he recognised how powerful an intellectual instrument is the instinctive knowledge of two languages, and was wont to insist upon the aid he had derived from Gaelic in the study of Hebrew and Latin. To one familiar with the complex and archaic organisation of Gaelic speech the acquisition of these languages must indeed be far easier than to one whose first knowledge of speech is based upon the analytic simplicity of English.

From the High School he gladly passed to College, where a happier life and more congenial friendships awaited him. He had many Highland fellow-students, and at this early date his love for the rich stores of oral tradition preserved by his countrymen manifested itself. He sought the acquaintance of good story-tellers, and began to store up in his keenly retentive memory the treasure he has been so largely instrumental in preserving and recording.

After leaving college he read law for awhile with Mr. Foulds. In his lonely island parish he later found his legal training of the utmost assistance. Many were the disputes he was called upon to settle, and, as he has recorded, few there were of his parishioners who needed to take the dangerous voyage to the Sheriff's court on a neighbouring island. At once judge and jury his decisions commanded respect and acquiescence. At this period, and for some time previously, his interest in and mastery of Gaelic lengendary lore are shown by the fact that he acted as Secretary to the Glasgow University Ossianic Society, founded in 1831 by *Caraid nan Gàidheal*, and still flourishing.

His thoughts and aspirations had early turned towards the church, and in 1858 he was licensed by the Presbytery of Glasgow. But suffering as he then was from the effects of inflammation of the lungs, the result of a chill caught in his student days, and the effects of which were perceptible throughout life, he was forbidden to preach for six months. The interval, spent in recruiting his shattered health, was profitable to his growing zeal for folk-lore studies. In Ayrshire or at Blair Athole he showed himself a keen and sympathetic collector of floating oral tradition.

In 1860 he accepted the appointment to the united parishes of Tiree and Coll from the Duke of Argyll, and took up the work which was to occupy the remaining thirty years of his life. It is to be wished that a sphere of activity more commensurate with his abilities had been accepted by him, as when he was offered the assistantship of St. Columba, Glasgow, and he seems at times to have felt as much. But such thoughts were certainly no hindrance to the performance of his duty, interpreted in the largest and most liberal sense. He was the guide and counsellor of his flock, who turned to him with unfailing confidence for advice, exhortation, or reproof. An amusing instance of his parishioners' belief in his capacity may be cited; a sailor lad from Tiree got, as sailor lads will, into some row in Spain and was marched off to jail. He took the matter philosophically, remarking, 'so long as the minister is alive I know they can't hurt me' *(bha fhios agam co fad's a bha'm ministear beò nach robh cunnart domh).* The esteem and affection in which he was held by his parishioners were cordially reciprocated by him. He is reported as saying that nowhere could be found a more intelligent community than the Duke's tenantry in Tiree, and in the preface to Volume IV. of the present series he bears witness to the knowledge, intelligence, and character of his informants.

We do not go far wrong in conjecturing that the minister's zealous interest for the preservation and elucidation of the native traditions was not the least potent of his claims upon the respect and love of his flock. How keenly the Highlander still treasures these faint echoes of the past glories and sorrows of his race is known to all who have won his confidence. Unhappily it has not always been the case that this sentiment has been fostered and turned to good account by the natural leaders of the people as it was by John Gregorson Campbell.

In the guidance of his people, in congenial study, in correspondence with Campbell of Islay and other fellow-workers, specimens of which will be found in the appendix *(infra* 138*),* time passed. His mother died in 1890 at the manse, and his health, for long past indifferent, broke down. The last years of his life were solaced and filled by the work he prepared for the present series. At last, Nov. 22nd, 1891 he passed from his labours and sufferings into rest, the rest of one who had well earned it by devotion to duty and to the higher interests of his race.

In person Campbell was tall and fair, with deep blue eyes full of life and vivacity. He was noted at once for the kindliness of his manner, and for the shrewd causticity of his wit. The portrait which serves as frontispiece is taken from the only available photograph, and represents him in middle life.

His Work as a Folk-Lorist.

The Gaels of Scotland cannot be accused of indifference to the rich stores of legend current among the people. From the days of the Dean of Lismore, in the late 15th century, onwards, there have not been wanting lovers and recorders of the old songs and stories. Unfortunately, in the 18th century, a new direction was given to the national interest in the race traditions by the Macpherson controversy. I say unfortunately, because attention was thereby concentrated upon one section of tradition to the neglect of others equally interesting and beautiful, and false standards were introduced into the appreciation and criticism of popular oral literature. Valuable as are the materials accumulated in the Report of the Highland Society, and generally in the voluminous literature which grew up round Macpherson's pretentions, they are far less valuable than they might be to the folk-lorist and student of the past, owing to the misapprehension of the real points both of interest and at issue. Two generations had to pass away before Scotch Gaelic folklore was to be studied and appreciated for itself.

To Campbell of Islay and the faithful fellow-workers whom he knew how to inspire and organise, falls the chief share in this work, belongs the chief honour of its successful achievement. The publication of the *Popular Tales of the West Highlands* was epoch-making, not only in the general study of folk-lore, but specially for the appreciation and intelligence of Gaelic myth and romance. No higher praise can be given to John Gregorson Campbell than that his folk-lore work is full of the same uncompromising fidelity to popular utterance, the same quick intuition into, and sympathetic grasp of popular imagination as Islay's. His published work has indeed a somewhat wider range than that of *Leabhar na Fèinne* and the *Popular Tales of the West Highlands*, as it deals also with those semi-historic traditions, the nearest equivalent the literature of these islands can show to the Icelandic family sagas, which Islay excluded from the two collections he issued. The following is a complete list, so far as can be ascertained, of the published writings of John Gregorson Campbell, in so far as they relate to the legendary romance, history and folk-lore of Gaelic Scotland.

HIGHLAND MONTHLY.

Vol. I. No. 10. p. 622, Introduction, &c.

WAIFS AND STRAYS OF CELTIC TRADITION.

Argyllshire Series, No. I. : The Good Housewife (p. 54-69).

Argyllshire Series, No. IV.: The Fians : or Stories, Poems, and
Traditions of Fionn and his Warrior Band. Collected entirely
from oral sources. 1891.

IN presenting his material to the English reader Campbell may
profitably be compared with Islay. In few ways was the
work of the latter more fruitful than in his mode of rendering
Gaelic into English. It is impossible, for instance, to look at
the work done of late by the distinguished Irish folk-lorists who
are adding a new chapter to Gaelic romance, at the work of
Douglas Hyde and W. Larminie and Jeremiah Curtin, and not
recognise how much in point of colour and tone and smack
of the soil their translations excel those of the pre-Campbell
generation. Islay may, at times, have pushed his theory of
idiomatic fidelity too far, occasionally where he aims at a
rendering he achieves a distortion, but as a whole the effect of
strange, wild, archaic atmosphere and medium is given with
unerring—one would call it skill, did one not feel that it is the
outcome of a nature steeped in the Gaelic modes of conception
and expression, and bold enough to invent the English requisite
to give an adumbration of them. For indeed the speech of
the *Popular Tales* is a distinctive variety of English, deserving
study both from the philologist and the artist in words. Islay
himself never handled this speech to better effect than did John
Gregorson Campbell in the fine tale, for instance, of Sir Olave
O'Corn *(Gaelic Soc. of Inverness,* Vol. XIII.*)*, or in the
Muileartach (Waifs and Strays, Vol. IV.*)*, though as a rule he
keeps closer than Islay to the ordinary standard of English
expression. Readers of this volume cannot fail to note the
exceeding skill with which the pithy, imaginative turns of
thought, so plentiful in the original, are rendered into English.

The reader is at once taken out of nineteenth century civilisation, and, which is surely the first thing required from the translator, by the mere sound and look of the words carried back into an older, wilder, simpler and yet, in some ways, more artificially complex life The difficulty of rendering Gaelic into English does not lie in the fact of its possessing a rude simplicity which the more sophisticated language is incapable of reproducing, but rather in that, whilst the emotions and conceptions are close to the primitive passions of nature in a degree that our civilisation has long forsworn, the mode of expression has the richness of colour and elaborate artificiality of a pattern in the Book of Kells. To neglect the latter characteristic is to miss not only a salient feature of the original but to obscure the significance of a dominant factor in the evolution of Gaelic artistry.

That Campbell, like Islay, felt the paramount necessity of endeavouring to reproduce the formal characteristics of his Gaelic text is certain; like Islay, he too, had the true scholar's regard for his matter. To put down what he heard, to comment upon what he found, was his practice. It seems obvious, but many collectors neglect it all the same. Nor in his essays at interpretation is he other than in full sympathy with his subject. He not only understands but himself possesses the mythopoeic faculty, and if this is endowed with a wider knowledge, a more refined culture than belonged to the Gaelic bards who first gave these songs and stories their present shape, or to the peasants and fishermen who lovingly repeat them, it differs in degree only, not in kind. It may be doubted that the framers of the *Muileartach* consciously embodied the conceptions which Campbell has read into the old poem *(Waifs and Strays*, IV. pp 131-135), but I think it certain that he does but give shape with the precision of a a higher culture to ideas which, with them, never emerged from the stage of mythic realisation.

THE PRESENT WORK.

MOST of the matter contained in the present volume had been partially, if not definitely, prepared for press by the author. The choice and arrangement are largely due to his sister, Mrs. Wallace, his devoted fellow-worker. Still it must not be forgotten that we have here a collection of posthumous remains which have not enjoyed the benefit of the author's final shaping and revision. But it has been judged best by the editors of the series to preserve these remains substantially as they were left, with a minimum of indispensable revision. The volume may lose in other respects, but it is, at all events, the work of the author and not of his editor friends. The latter have felt that regard for the genuineness of Mr. Campbell's text was the first of their duties towards his memory.

This volume thus represents the contents of Campbell's note-books rather than provides such an ordered collection of material, bearing upon a particular section of Gaelic folk-lore, as he has furnished in the preceding volume of this series. But for this very reason it yields better evidence to the wealth and variety of Gaelic popular tradition. A large portion of the book is local legendary matter, and is closely analogous to what the Icelandic Sagas must have been in one stage of their development, a stage overlaid by the artistry of a greater school of prose story tellers than ever took the sagas of Gaelic Scotland in hand. Professor York Powell has well analysed the phase through which such stories as those of Burnt Njal or Egil Skallagrimm's son must have passed before they reached the form familiar to us.* He describes the popular narrator working up a mass of local, fairly authentic detail about his hero, running it into a conventional mould, and then fitting the result into a scheme of wider historic scope. The Gaelic matter preserved alike by Mr. Campbell in this volume and by

---

* Folk-Lore, June, 1894.

Mr. MacDougall in the first volume of the series has not got beyond the local anecdote stage, though, as in the variant forms of the tale of the Grizzled Lad and MacNeill (p. 5, *et seq.*), we can see the conventionalizing process at work, accentuating certain details, discarding others, with the view of transmuting the blurred photographic variety of life into the clear-cut unity of art. But the process is rudimentary. It is strange that this should be so considering the wealth of conventional situations that lay ready to the hand of the Gaelic story teller in the highly elaborated sagas of Cuchulainn and of Finn, for the purpose of moulding the achievements of historical Campbells, MacLeans and MacNeills, into a satisfactory artistic form. Such convention as is apparent in these scraps of sagas is related to that of the folk-tale rather than to that of the great heroic legends. An interesting example is afforded by the story of Mac an Uidhir. This may well have a basis of fact, indeed Campbell cites an actual analogue, but it has been run into the shape of an ordinary separation and timely-recognition folk-tale. Other instances will present themselves to the reader and afford instructive study of the action and reaction upon each other of folk-life and oral narrative legend.

Any fresh addition of moment to the considerable recorded mass of Scottish local historic tradition increases the wonder that material of such vigour and interest, full of the clash of fierce primitive passion, rich in character, should have had so little literary outcome. The stuff is not inferior to that of the Icelandic tales, but instead of a first-rate contribution to the world's literature we have only a chaos of unworked up details. Yet during the time that these implanted themselves and took shape in the popular memory, Gaelic story-tellers, elaborating and perpetually readapting the old mythic and heroic traditions of the race, were producing narratives of rare and exquisite charm. Perplexity is intensified if, as Professor Zimmer maintains, the Norsemen learnt the art of prose narrative from the Irish and developed the great school of Icelandic story telling on lines picked up in Gaeldom. Certain it is that the Irish annals, relating the events of the 3rd to 9th centuries, which assumed their present shape sometime in the 10th to the 12th centuries, contain a large amount of historic narrative that is closely allied in form and spirit to the contemporary Scotch Gaelic sagas. There is the same directness of narrative, the frequent picturesqueness of incident, the pithy characterisation ; there is also the same failure to throw the material into a rounded artistic form, and, most curious of all resemblances, the conventions at work distorting historic fact are those of the folk-tale rather than of the national heroic epos. I would cite in this connection certain episodes of the Boroma* (in itself an admirable example of the failure of Gaelic story tellers to work up into satisfying form very promising historical material) such as that of Cumascach's visit to Brandubh, or again many passages in the stories about Raghallach and Guaire. The whole subject is, as nearly everything else in the record of Gaelic letters, fraught with fascinating perplexities. The present writer can but here, as he has so often done before, make a big note of interrogation and trust that Gaelic scholars on both sides the water will consider the problem worth study, and succeed in solving it.

I note those points which interest me as a student of tradition in general, and of Celtic tradition in particular. For most readers these scraps of local history derive their chief value from the vivid light they flash back upon the past, from the evidence they yield of the wild, fierce—I had almost written savage—life from which we are separated by so few generations.

---

* The *Boroma*, the story of the tribute imposed upon Leinster by Tuathal Techtmar in the second century and remitted in the sixth century, has been edited and translated by Mr. Whitley Stokes, *(Rev. Celt.)* and by Mr. Standish Hayes O'Grady in *Silva Gadelica*.

Some there may be to mourn for the past. Not a few Highland landlords will possibly regret the good old days when the MacLean planted his gallows in the midst of the island of Tiree, and the last comer with his rent knew what awaited him (p. 13). Truly a more effectual means of getting in the money than by writ which the sheriff cannot execute.

The remainder of the volume comprises matter more upon the usual folk-lore lines ; much, familiar already but valuable in the good variant form here recorded, much again novel, like the curious tale of the Princess Thyra and her lovers. Taken in conjunction with the author's previous volume in this series on the Finn tradition as still living in the Western Highlands, the whole offers a faithful picture of the imagination, memory, and humour of the Gaelic peasant playing round the old-time beliefs, stories and customs handed down to him from his forefathers.

ALFRED NUTT.

I append a list of the chief informants from whom Mr. Campbell derived the material contained in Vol. IV. and V. of the Argyllshire series of *Waifs and Strays of Celtic Tradition.*

> Malcolm MacDonald, Scarnish, Tiree.
> Malcolm MacLean, Kilmoluaig, Tiree.
> Hugh MacDonald,   do.   do.
> John MacLean, (bard), Balemartin, Tiree.
> Hugh Macmillan, (tailor), Tobermory.
> Angus MacVurrich, Portree, Skye.
> Duncan Cameron, (constable), Tiree.
> Allan MacDonald, Mannal, Tiree.
> Donald Mackinnon, Balevoulin, Tiree.
> John Cameron, *(Iain MacFhearchar)*, Balevoulin, Tiree.
> Archibald Mackinnon, *(Gilleasbuig ruadh nan sgeirean dubha)*, Tiree.
> Donald Cameron, Ruaig, Tiree.
> Donald Macdonald, Mannal, Tiree.
> Malcolm Sinclair, Balephuil, Tiree.
> John MacArthur, (tailor), Moss, Tiree.
> Duncan MacDonald, Caolis, Tiree.
> Neil MacLean, (the elder), Cornaig, Tiree.

CLAN TRADITIONS.

MACLEANS OF DOWART.

THE first MacLeans, Wily Lachlan *(Lachunn Lùbanach)*, and Punctilious Hector *(Eachann Reanganach)*, came to Dunolly to MacDougall. He sent them provisions and made his men watch to see if they were gentlemen. It was inferred they were, from their paring cheese, or, throwing the remains of their food to the dogs. On leaving Dunolly they came to Aros in Mull. This word Aros is the one regularly used to denote a royal residence or palace, and the Lords of the Isles claiming an independent sovereignty, their residence in Mull came to be called Aros, a name which it still retains. Their residence in the north was Duntulm, and in the Sound of Mull, Aros and Ardtornish. The view from the old castle of Aros up and down the Sound is very commanding, and that from Ardtornish is equally so. The MacLeans on coming to Aros found *Peddle Mòr* (a south country ploughman to *MacConnuill* of the Isles) who sent them food, but gave no knife and fork, telling them to put hen's bills on *(guib-chearc)* to take it. On coming to him they found him bending to repair a failing in the plank board *(fàillinn na fliuch-bhùird)*, or keel board, of a galley *(birlinn)* with which he was to go to meet his master.

The Lords of the Isles to make their estate appear greater employed, from the name, evidently a south countryman at agricultural work, hence the name Peddle which is not of Highland origin. They struck off his head and went themselves to meet MacConnuill whom they took prisoner, and brought to MacDougall. He however would take nothing to

A

do with the captive. At the advice of an old man they then returned with their prisoner to Aros, and got him pledged to give his daughter to one of them. Lachlan married the daughter and got Dowart.

It is said by some that Hector was the oldest of the two brothers, and that when MacCónnuill the Lord of the Isles was out pleasure-sailing with his daughter, the brothers overtook his galley and seizing him said "The omen of your capture has overtaken you" (" *Tha manadh do ghlacaidh ort* "). He had no ransom to offer but his daughter and lands. Lachlan took the daughter, and with her he got the lands of Dowart. The other got the lands of Lochbuy. MacCónnuill gave for food to the child born of the Dowart marriage Little Hernisker with its twenty-four islands (*Earnasgeir bheag le 'cuid eileanan*). Afterwards, at Ardtornish, the fourth or fifth descendant of Dowart asked the then Lord of the Isles for a livelihood (*màthair bheathachaidh*). He got the reply, "Jump the wall where it is lowest" (" *Leum an gàradh far an ìsle e* ") which led to Ardgour being taken from MacMaster, who was known at the time to be no favourite with the Lord of the Isles, and the attack made upon his land was readily commuted into a chartered possession. The tradition is as follows :

The Lord of the Isles was lying sick at Ardtornish. The MacCónnuill, now commonly called MacDonald, claimed a jurisdiction independent of the Scottish Crown till about 1493 A.D. or thereabouts, and many if not all the chiefs of the Western Highlands and Islands paid him court. Among others MacMaster, chief, or proprietor, of Ardgour, came to pay his respects at that time. Ventilation was not then so much regarded in the case of the sick as it is now, and MacMaster, being offended at some breath from the sick chamber, said *Fùich, fùich,* an expression of disgust and offence. Unfortunately for himself the inadvertent expression was made a handle of, and was never forgiven to MacMaster by the Lord of the Isles. In consequence, when the Laird of Dowart, who was married to a near relative of his, came to ask for a means of livelihood *(màthair bheathachaidh)* to the child born of his marriage with the kinswoman of the Lord of the Isles, the potentate said to him, "Jump the wall where it is lowest" *(Leum an gàradh far an ìsle e)*. The youth or young man being now of age to shift for himself, a company of men and a boat was given him by his father, and he made for Ardgour. A battle was then fought and MacMaster was defeated. One of MacMaster's sons, who was surnamed the Fox *(An sionnach)*, possibly because weakness often seeks to protect itself by wiliness and deceit or any other artifice that will give protection. In these stormy days any such means were more excusable. The Fox made his way to go across at Corran to the mainland after the battle. His father's fisherman was then fishing in the neighbourhood of the ferry at Red Bay *(Port Dearg)*, and the Fox called to him to ~~throw~~ him across to the other side. The fisherman who rejoiced in the caco-phonous name of Carrascally *(Mac-a-Charrusglaich)*, was deaf to his cry, and he only said that the cuddie fish was taking well *("Gu 'n robh gabhail mhaith air na cudainnean")* or that he lost his oars, and the young MacMaster had to hide himself in the adjoining wood. When the MacLeans came to the place, Carrascally said that there was a fox of the MacMasters still hiding in the wood, and the MacLeans pursued him. The cairn, or heap of stones, is still shown where the Fox was overtaken and slain.

Some say it was MacMaster himself, and not his son, who was flying after the defeat by the MacLeans, and was refused to be ferried by the fisherman, and that his son who was called the Fox, and had committed some fraud when abroad, was caught in Inverscaddel wood and was stabbed by MacLean.

The fisherman, who was rascally in more than name, came to MacLean and made claim to having done good service in having refused to help the fugitive; and in having pointed out that he was still in the wood. MacLean upon this put up three oars and made a gallows with them, on which he hanged the fisherman, or Carrascally, at the hangman's cove *(Port-a-chrochaire)*, saying if he had treated his master as he said he had done, it might be his turn another day, and the fisherman's cunning recoiling upon himself has passed into a proverb "The officiousness, or discretionary power of MacCarrascally chasing MacMaster's Fox," *("Meachanus Mhic a' Charrasglaich ruith Sionnach Mhic a' Mhaighstir")*. The MacLeans have ever since retained Ardgour, and have been esteemed for their position as Highland proprietors. Their title, in Gaelic is *Mac-'Ic-Eoghain* (the son of the son of Hugh). The son of the son of, or grandson, *(Mac-'Ic-)* being the word used in the Highlands of Scotland as the patronymic of Chiefs, instead of the O, or Grandson, used in Ireland, as O' Donnell, O' Brian, O' Meagher, &c. Thus, the son of the son of Patrick *(Mac-'Ic-Phàdruig)* denotes Grant of Glenmoriston; the son of the son of Alexander *(Mac-'Ic-Alasdair)*, the Chief of Glengarry; son of the son of Hector *(Mac-'Ic-Eachuinn)*, MacLean who had once Kingairloch. The title of some Chiefs is only son of *(Mac)*; as, Lochiel is known as the son of Dark Donald *(Mac Dho'uil Duibh)*. The leading Highland Chief is known as *Mac Cailein* (the son of Colin). The House of Argyll derives its Gaelic title from Colin, who was slain in a clan feud at the battle on the mountain known as the String of Lorn *(An t-Sreang Lathurnach)* when the ford, known as the Red Ford *(Ath Dearg)*, ran red with blood.

DEATH OF BIG LACHLAN MACLEAN, CHIEF OF DUART,—

(*Lachunn Mòr Dhuart*).

THE Chiefs of Duart were among the most powerful and influential chiefs in the Highlands. Their power was absolute, bearing the control of neither King nor Parliament, and there are many stories shewing that they were very unsparing in visiting with their vengeance, and even taking the lives of those who offended them.

A very notorious sea-robber and land plunderer of whom there are many tales in the Isle of Skye raised a *creach*, or cattle-spoil, from Macdonald Lord of the Isles, who then occupied a fort on the site of the present manse of Kilchoman in Islay. He managed also to circulate a report that it was the MacLeans from Mull who were the depredators. At that time MacLean, Duart, was ambitious to be overlord of a great part of Islay, and *Lachunn Mòr* came with a band of followers to Gruinard beach in the neighbourhood of the fort.

It is said that before leaving Mull, he was standing on the roof of Aros Castle which overlooks the Sound of Mull and on its being pointed out that an expedition to Islay would be very dangerous to his men, he said, that he did not care though there should not be a MacLean in Mull except those descended from himself. Neither he himself nor his men came back from the ill-fated expedition. After landing at Gruinard beach (*Tràigh Ghrunnard*) he was met by the Macdonalds. A little man, known in tradition as the Black Elf (*Dubh Sìth*) and (*Ochd-rann bodaich*), or eighth part of a man—[In Scotch the eighth part would be the lippie used for measuring grain and meal. According to the table to be found in old Reckoning Books a boll consists of two pecks and each peck of four lippies.

This makes each lippie equal to an eighth part of a boll],—
offered his services for the battle to MacLean, but the haughty
Chief rejected the offer with disdain. The Black Elf then
went to MacDonald, who accepted his offer; and during all the
current of the heady fight the dwarf was observed to follow
MacLean for an opportunity to kill him with an arrow. An
opportunity having at last occurred by MacLean lifting his
arm, an arrow was launched and MacLean was pierced on the
side, and fell with a deadly wound. Having lost their Chief
the MacLeans were routed with loss, and those who escaped
from the battle, having taken refuge in a neighbouring church,
were destroyed by the MacDonalds, who set the church on fire.
The body of Lachunn Mòr was taken on a sledge, there being
no wheeled vehicles in those days, to Kilchoman burying-
ground. Some say that the person who took him was his wife,
and others say it was his foster-mother. His head from the
motion of the sledge nodded in a manner that made the boy
who accompanied her laugh. She was so much offended at his
ill-timed merriment that she took a sword and killed him on
the spot. The site of this tragedy in Benviger is still pointed
out and the place where Lachunn Mòr himself was buried
is known to the people of the place although no headstone
marks it.

THE Laird of Dowart was on his way to gather rent in Tiree, and sent ashore to Kelis *(Caolas)*, Coll, for meat *(biadhtachd)*. The woman of the house told MacLean was not worth sending meat to, and Dowart kindly came ashore to see why she said so. She said it because he was not taking Coll for himself. Three brothers from Lochlin had Coll at the time, Big Annla *(Annla Mòr)* in Loch Annla, another in *Dun bithig* in Totronald, and the third in Grisipol hill. She had thirty men herself fit to bear arms. Dowart went to Loch Annla fort late in the evening alone, and was hospitably received. Annla's arrows were near the fire, and Dowart gradually edged near them till he managed to make off with them. This led to a fight at Grimsari and is perhaps the reason why Dowart encouraged *Iain Garbh* to make himself master of Coll.

Stout John *(Iain Garbh)* was fourth MacLean,—others say the first of Coll. When nine or twelve months old, his mother, having become a widow, had married MacNeill of Barra, *Iain Garbh* was sent by his step-father to Barra, in charge of a nurse *(ban-altruim)*. This woman was courted by a Barraman, whom, as her charge was a pretty boy, she at first refused. Her lover, however, got word that *Iain Garbh* was to be killed at MacNeill's instigation, and told her. The three fled, in a boat with two oars, from Barra during night. An eight-oared galley *(ochd ràmhach)*, with a steersman set off in chase. At Sorisdale in Coll, beyond Eilereig, in the borderline *(crìch)* between Sorisdale and Boust, there is a narrow sound, for which both boats were making, and the little one was almost overtaken. It was overtake and not overtake *(beir 's cha bheir)*.

The little boat went through the sound *(caolas)* safely, but the oars of the large boat were broken. Hence, 'The Sound of Breaking Oars' *(Caolas 'Bhriste-Ràmh)* is the name of the Sound to this day. The little boat put to sea again, and was lost to sight. The Barra men went to every harbour near, "The Wooded Bay" *(Bàgh na Coille)* &c., where they thought it might come, but they never saw it again. It is supposed it went to Mull. There is no further mention of the Barra man or the nurse. Stout John *(Iain Garbh)* went to Ireland, and when well grown told the woman with whom he stayed that he had a dream of a pile of oaten cakes *(tòrr de bhonnaich choirce)* and a drip from the roof *(boinne snithe)*, had fallen and gone right through them. The woman said the dream meant he was a laird of land *(ceannard fearainn)* and would get back his own. On this he came to Mull, and having got men, of whom seven were from Dervaig, the baldheaded black fellow, *(gille maol dubh)* afterwards known as Grizzled Lad *(Gille Riabhach)* being one of them with him, went to Coll. His companions vowed to kill whatever living *(beò)* they fell in with first, after landing in Coll. Stout John *(Iain Garbh)* had a mark on the forehead by his having fallen on the edge of an iron pot.

His fostermother *(muime)* was gathering shellfish *(buain maoraich)*. He went to speak to her, when he came behind her as she stumbled, and she exclaimed, "God be with MacLean" *("Dia le Mac-'illeathain")*, "My loss that MacLean is not alive" *("Mo sgaradh nach bu mhairionn do Mhac-'illeathain")*. When pressed to explain herself she said, "Conceal what I said: many an unfortunate word women say" *("Dean rùn maith orm : is ioma facal tubaisdeach their na mnathan")*, and at last he told her his story. It had been long foretold that he would return. The Mull men came up, and the Grizzled Lad *(Gille Riabhach)* was going to kill the woman, according to the vow. Stout John *(Iain Garbh)* told who she was, and her life was spared. She informed them that MacNeill sent a servant every day from Grisipol House, where his headquarters were, to Breacacha for news. If all was well, the messenger was to return riding slowly with his face to the horse's tail; if any one returned with him, a friend was to walk on the right of the horse, a stranger *(fogarach)* on the left; and she said that he had just left on his way home. Stout John *(Iain Garbh)* and his companions left the Hidden Anchorage *(Acarsaid Fhalaich)* and went to the top of the place called Desert *(Fàsach)*. They there saw the rider of the white horse at Arileòid. Stout John *(Iain Garbh)* promised reward to any one who would intercept him, before he reachd Grisipol. The Grizzled Lad *(Gille Riabhach)* said he would do so, if he got Dervaig, his native place, rent free. MacLean promised this, but the lad said, "Words may be great till it comes to solemn oaths" *(Is mòr briathran gun lughadh)*, and made him swear to the deed. The Grizzled Lad *(Gille Riabhach)* set off, and above the Broad Knoll *(Cnoc Leathan)* saw the horseman at the township of Hough. When at the Stone of Moaning *(Clach Ochanaich)*, on the top of Ben Hough, he saw him past Clabbach. He made for the road, near the present Free Church Manse, and lay down, and pretending to be a beggar began to hunt through his clothes. Where the Little Cairn of the King's Son *(Carnan mhic an Righ)* stands, the horseman came up, was pulled off his horse and killed. The lad then waited till his companions came up, and proceeded to Grisipol with two on each side. It was dinner time, and his servant the Black Lad *(Gille Dubh)* brought word to MacNeill of the party coming. His wife, looking out of an opening, said one of the party coming looked like her son. MacNeill exclaimed, "War time is not a time for sleep" *("Cha-n àm cadal an cogadh")*, and went out to give battle. In the fight the Grizzled Lad *(Gille Riabhach)* was hard pressed by the Black Lad, *(Gille Dubh)*, and sideways jumped the stream that runs past Grisipol House at the place still known as the Grizzly Lad's leap *(Leum a' Ghille Riabhaich)* to avoid the blow of the battle-axe. The axe stuck in the ground, and before it was recovered, the Grizzly Lad *(Gille Riabhach)*, jumping back, threw off the Black Lad's *(Gille Dubh)* head. Stout John *(Iain Garbh)* was hard pressed by MacNeill himself, and both were out in the sea at the foot of the stream.

"Disgrace on you MacLean, though it is enough that you are being driven by the son of the skate-eating carl" *("Miapadh ort, a Mhic 'illeathainn, 's leoir tha thu gabhail iomain roimh Mhac bodach nan sgat")*, said the Grizzly Lad *(Gille Riabhach)* coming up to them, and then calling to MacNeill, "I am not in a mood to deceive you, there they are behind you" *("Cha bhi mi'm brath fville dhuit, sin iad agad air do chùlthaobh")*, and when MacNeill turned round the Grizzly Lad *(Gille Riabhach)* threw off his head with the axe. The MacNeills fled and were beset and killed in the Hollow of bones *(Slochd-nan-cnàmh)* in the lower part of Grisipol Hill *(Iochdar Beinn Ghrisipol)*. They then returned to Grisipol, and MacNeill's widow, Stout John's *(Iain Garbh's)* mother, held up her child a suckling *(ciocharan)*, that Stout John *(Iain Garbh)* might spare him and acknowledge his own half-brother. He was for sparing it, but the Grizzly Lad *(Gille Riabhach)* told him to put the needle on the ploughshare *(cuir an t-snathad air a' choltar)*. The child was killed.

An additional if not a different account is :

Stout John *(Iain Garbh)* first of Coll, when a boy, was obliged to fly from Coll to Dowart, and his mother married MacNeill of Barra. When he came of age, and was for making good his claim to his native island, in raising the clan he came to a widow's house in Dervaig. She said her other sons were away, or they would be at his service, and she had only a big stripling of a grizzly looking lad *(Stiall mòr de ghille riabhach)* if he choose to take him. He took him, and it was well for him he did. It is said that this family of whom the

Grizzly Lad *(Gille Riabhach)* was one, and whose services were at MacLean's command, were Campbells. MacNeill kept a man with a white horse at Arinagour, and if the MacLeans were heard to land in the island, he was to ride off at full speed to Breacacha. If anything was wrong the messenger was to turn his head to the horse's tail when he came in sight of Breacacha. The Grizzly Lad *(Gille Riabhach)* took across the hill, where there is now a straight road, and intercepted this rider. On hearing from him that MacNeill was at Grisipol, he suddenly leapt behind him on the horse, and killed him with his dirk. He rode back to his own party, and then slowly to Grisipol where the MacNeills were at dinner.

MacLean and his men were faint and weary for want of food. They had not tasted anything since they left Mull. They entered a tenant's house and asked food. The man had nothing for them, once he had enough, but since the MacLeans had left the island, he had come to grief and poverty. He said to Stout John *(Iain Garbh)* his heart warmed to him, he was so like his ancient masters. On learning who they were he gave all the milk he had to them.

At the fight at Grisipol, the Grizzly Lad *(Gille Riabhach)* was hard pressed by MacNeill's body servant, who was armed with a battle-axe. On the margin of the stream, as the axe was raised to strike down, he leaped backwards, and upwards, across the stream, and the place of the leap is still known as the 'Grizzly Lad's leap' *(Leum a' Ghille Riabhaich)*. The axe went into the ground, and before MacNeill's man could defend himself the Grizzly Lad *(Gille Riabhach)* jumped back and threw off his head.

Stout John *(Iain Garbh)* himself was hard pressed by MacNeill, and driven to the beach. The Grizzly Lad *(Gille Riabhach)* came to his rescue. MacNeill's wife cried out to Stout John *(Iain Garbh)* her son by her first marriage, that his enemies were coming behind him. The Grizzly Lad *(Gille*

Riabhach) called out to him to watch his enemies in front, and he would watch those behind.

MacNeill and his men were killed. The Grizzly Lad *(Gille Riabhach)* said he would take to flight and pretend to be one of the MacNeills, of whom another party was coming to the rescue from Breacacha. He fled and made signals to the MacNeills to fly. They fled to a cave near the Hidden Anchorage *(Acarsaid fhalaich)* where their bones are still to be seen.

When Stout John *(Iain Garbh)* entered Grisipol house, his mother stood before him with a child, his half brother, on her shoulder. She told him to look at his young brother smiling at him. Stout John *(Iain Garbh)* was for sparing the infant but the Grizzly Lad *(Gille Riabhach)* warned him, the child if spared to come of age would avenge his father's death, and he himself stabbed the infant with his dirk on his mother's shoulder.

BROWNS OF TIREE.
(Clann-a-Bhruthain).

THE Browns of Tiree at the present day are called *Brunaich,* sing. *Brunach,* evidently a word not of native origin, and likely an adaptation of the English Brown. Brown as the name of a colour is an English word but not Gaelic, the Gaelic for it being *donn,* hence as a clan name many affirm that the Brown of the present day is a corruption or modification of *Bruthainn* certainly the older name, and till very recently, the name given to a sept or portion of the Browns. There are also many who maintain that the oldest form of all is *Mac-'ill-duinn.*

Other explanations are also put forward in behalf of the origin of the name, but none of them are satisfactorily conclusive. The following story of how the Browns came first to Tiree is a tradition as like to be true as any other. It was heard from a native of the island, well acquainted with the traditions of his countrymen.

The wife of MacLean of Dowart was a daughter of the Lord of the Isles. Her father on visiting her at Aros had found her destitute of table-linen, and on her being spoken to on the subject, she said that there was no place on the estate where lint could be grown. Her father then gave her the island of Tiree as a good flax-growing country, that she might not be open to that reproach any longer. In this way the island of Tiree remained in the possession of the Dowart family till the forfeiture of the clan towards the end of the seventeenth century. The MacLeans seem to have ruled the island with a rod of iron. There is still shewn the hillock called the Bank of the Gallows *(Bac na Croiche)*, where the man who came in last with his rent at collection time was hanged. A party of strong men called 'MacLean's attributes' *(buaidheanan Mhic-'illeathain)* but more correctly oppressors and bullies, were kept in the island to overawe the people.

This wife of Dowart, with her galley and men, was at Croig in Mull, awaiting for a passage across to Tiree. When the men were getting the galley in order, a big strong man was observed making his way to the boat, His appearance was that of a beggar, with tattered and patched garments *(lùirichean)*. He quietly asked to be allowed a passage with them. The master of the boat gruffly refused, saying, that they would not allow one like him to be in the same boat with their mistress, but the beggar said that his being there would make no difference, and asked the favour of getting a passage from her. She gave him permission and he seated himself at the end of the boat furthest from her to avoid giving trouble to her. The day was becoming boisterous; it was not long till the master said that the wind was becoming too high, and the day unlikely. A heavy sea was shipped wetting the Lady of Dowart, and the beggar said to the master, "Can you not steer better than that?" The master said "Could you do better?" The beggar replied "It would not be difficult for me to do better than that at any rate. Show me the direction where you wish to go," and on it being shewn to him he added "I think you may go on that you will make land."

"What do you know?" the other said, "it is none of your business to speak here."

The Lady then spoke, and said to the beggar, "Will you take the boat there if you get the command of it?" He said he would, and she gave orders to let him have the command. He sat at the helm and told them to shorten sail, and make everything taut, and now, the boat did not take in a thimbleful of water. They made for Tiree, and the place come to was the lower part of Hynish, at the furthest extremity of the island. The first place of shelter which the beggar saw, he let the boat in there. The little cove is still known as the Port of the Galley *(Port-na-Birlinn)* on the south side of *Barradhu* where the present dwellings belonging to the Skerryvore Light-house are. The company landed safely, and on parting the Lady of Dowart told the beggar man to come to see her at Island House, where the residence of the Dowart family was at that time, and which is still the proprietory residence of the island. The name Island House is derived from its present site having been formerly surrounded by the water of the fresh-water lake near it. It communicated with the rest of the island by means of a draw-bridge, but there being now no necessity for this safeguard the space between the house and the shore has been filled up, and the moated grange has become like ordinary dwelling houses. The stranger wandered about for some time, and then went to the Island House and was kindly received. After a day or two, he thought it would be better to get a house for himself, and the Lady of Dowart said that she would give him any place that he himself would fix upon. Apparently the island was not much tenanted then, and according to the custom of the time, he got a horse with a pack-saddle on, and on the ridge of the saddle *(cairb na srathrach)*, he put the upper and lower stones of a quern *(bràthuinn)*, one on each side of the horse, secured by a straw, or sea-bent rope, and wherever the rope broke it was lucky to build the house there. The beggar-man's quern fell at Sunny Spot *(Grianal)*, now better known as Greenhill. He built a bothy there, and a woman came to keep house for him. By her he had a son, whom he would not acknowledge. When the child was able to take care of itself she went again to him with it that she might be free. He still refused to receive the child and told her to avoid him. She then thought as she had heard from him before where he came from, that she would go with her son to his relatives in Ireland. When she arrived there the child's grandfather received her very kindly. She stayed with him till her son had grown to manhood *(gus an robh e 'na làn duine)*. As she was about to return the grandfather said to his grandson, "Which do you now prefer, to follow your mother, or stay with me?" The lad said he would rather follow his mother, and risk his fortune along with her. They came back to Tiree again, and the son would give no rest till they went to see his father. When they reached the bothy the mother said "you will surely receive your son to-day though you would not acknowledge him before." But he would not any more than at first. His son then took hold of him, and putting his knee on his breast, said, "before you rise from there you will own me as your lawful son, and my mother as your married wife." He did this and was set free. They then lived together and built a house, and houses, and increased in stock of cattle. One wild evening in spring, when they were folding the cattle, they observed a stout looking man of mean appearance coming from Kilkenneth, still a township in that part of the island, and making straight for the house.

"I never saw a bigger man than that beggar," said the son.

"He is big," the father said, "I well know what man it is; he is coming after me, and I will lose my life this night, I killed his brother, but it was not my fault, for if I had not killed him, he would have killed me."

"Perhaps you will not lose your life to-night yet," said the son, "be kind to him, and when he has warmed himself, ask him to go out with us to kill a cow, for the night is cold."

The stranger came in and was made welcome. The old man then said since there was a stranger, and the night chilly, they better take a cow and kill it. They went out and brought in the cow. The young man said to the stranger, "Which would you rather, take the axe, or hold the cow's horn?" *(Co dhiu b' fhearr leis an tuath na 'n adharc)*. The stranger chose to hold the horn, and the blow by which the beast was felled was so sudden and unexpected that the stranger fell with it. The youth immediately fell upon him and kept him down, saying, "You will only have what you can do for yourself, till you tell why you came here to-night *(Cha bhi agad ach na bheir thu g'a chionn gus an aidich thu 'de thug so an nochd thu)*. He told word for word how he came to avenge his brother's death. *(Dh' innis e facal air an fhacal mar thainig e thoirt mach èirig a bhràthair)*.

"You will not leave this alive" said the young man, "until you promise not to molest my father while you remain in the country." The stranger vowed, if released he would not offend anyone. He was allowed to remain and they passed the night cheerfully and peacefully *(gu sona sàmhach)*. The stranger returned the way he came. The father and son then settled together, and are said according to tradition, to have been the first Browns in Tiree.

Another version of the story is, that the first settler in Greenhill was a Campbell, and that he was the maker of those underground dwellings *(tighean falaich)* which still exist on that farm; curious habitations, which are unlike any building now in use, and worthy of closer examination by antiquarians. It is said that there are buildings with similar entrances exposed by sand blowing and covered with a great depth of earth in Tra-vi at the distance of two miles or more further south.

There is a precipice on the west side of Kenavara hill called Mac-a-Bhriuthainn's leap *(Leum Mhic-a-bhriuthainn)* which one of this sept of Browns is said to have jumped across backwards, and which no one has since jumped either backwards or forwards. The one who took the jump is said to have been chased by a wild ox, which pushed him over the hill, and if he had not been a man of steady eye and limb, the fall would have ended in sure destruction. The place where he leapt was a ledge in the face of a precipice where the slightest over-balance or weakness, would have precipitated him several hundred feet into a dangerous and deep sea. No trained tight-rope dancer ever required more sureness of eye and limb than must have been brought into action in this leap.

In the top of the same hill (Kenavara) there is a well, Briuthainn's Well *(Tobar Mhic-a-Bhriuthainn)*, which is said to have its name from the first who came to the island having, in his wanderings, subsisted on its water and wild water-cress.

THE STORY OF MAC-AN-UIDHIR.

THE name Mac-an-Uidhir is not borne by any person now living, so far as the writer is aware. Like many other names it may have been changed into MacDonald, or some other clan-name. When a person changed his name to that of some other clan, or powerful chief, he was said to accept the name and clanship *(Ainm 'sa chinneadhdas).* This name must, at one time, however, have been common. The ford between Benbecula and South Uist is called "The ford of the daughter of Euar" *(Faoghail Nic an Uidhir),* and Nic-an-Uidhir is also named by the Lochnell bard as a sister of Headless Stocking *(Cas-a'-Mhogain),* a well-known witch, who lived so long ago as when Ossian the poet was a boy *(giullan).*

" Did ever you hear mention
Of Rough Foot-gear daughter of Euar ?
She was young in Glenforsa,
When Ossian was a young boy ;
She was going about as a slip of a girl
With Headless Stocking her sister.
I am a wretched creature after them
Not knowing what became of them."

("An cuala sibhse riamh iomradh
Mu Chaiseart Gharbh, Nic an Uidhir ?
Bha i òg an Gleann Forsa
Nar bha Oisean 'na ghiullan ;
Bha i falbh 's i 'na proitseach
Le Cas-a'-Mhogain a piuthar.
'S mise an truaghan 'nan déigh
'S gun fhios gu de thainig riu.")

The person of whom the following story is told, lived at Hynish in the island of Tiree, and had become engaged to a young woman in the neighbourhood. Between the espousal and marriage, the engaged couple went with a party of friends for a sail to Heisker, near Canna. The men of the party went ashore seal-hunting and one of the young woman's disappointed suitors took advantage of the opportunity to get Mac-an-Uidhir left behind, and coming back to the boat told that the intending bridegroom had been drowned. By this lie he hoped to make the bride despair of seeing her intended any more, and by renewing his own attentions, to get her to consent to accept himself. She, however, not believing that he was dead, said that she would marry no one for a year and a day from the date of his alleged drowning. [Heisker means high rock,* and this one, near the island of Canna, is called the High Rock of Windlestraws *(Heisgeir nan Cuiseag)*. It has no one living on it. At the present day a few young cattle are grazed upon it, and a boat comes for them in spring from Canna, which lies to the N.E. It is not otherwise visited except once or twice a year by seal-hunters.]

At first, Mac-an-Uidhir subsisted on birds and fish eaten raw ; after his powder and shot were expended, he had to keep himself alive upon whelks, or whatever he could get along the shore, principally whelks. This sort of shellfish is said to keep a person alive though he should have no other means of subsistence, till he becomes as black as the shield or wing of the whelk *(co dubh ri sgiath faochaig)*. The abandoned and castaway youth lived in this way for three quarters of a year ; but at last he got away from the islet, and for the last three months of the year was making his way home. He arrived on the night on which the marriage of his intended to his

---

* The islet near North Uist, on which the Mona Light house is built, is called the High Rock of the Monks, *Heisgeir nam Manach.*

unscrupulous rival was to take place. He went to the house of his foster-mother, who did not know him, his appearance through his privations having becoming so much changed, and, he having asked to be allowed to remain for the night, she said she was alone, and could not let a stranger like him stay. She also told of the festivities in the neighbourhood, and said that he had better pass the night there. He asked the occasion of the festivities: she told him how her foster-son had been drowned, and supplanted, and that this was the night of his rival's marriage, saying, "If they are happy I am sad, another one being in the place of my foster-son" *(Ma tha iadsan subhach tha mise dubhach dheth, fear eile bhi dol an àite mo dhalta)*. She then added, "this time last year, he perished when he went with a party to hunt seals in Heisker; his intended vowed that she would not marry for a year, in the hope of his returning, as she had not been quite satisfied that he had been drowned, and to-night the time is expired." "Let us go'" he said, "to see them."

"You may go," she replied, "but they are near enough to me as it is." He then asked her if she did not recognise him, and told who he was, but she refused to believe him, saying her dear child *(mo ghràdh)* could not be so much altered in the time. He put the matter out of question by asking if she would know her own handiwork, and shewing what was left of the hose *(osain)* she had given him, to convince her. When she saw the labour of her own hands *(saothair a làmh fhéin)*, she joyfully welcomed him, and went with him where the marriage party were. Those who were there were surprised to see her arrival, knowing the sad state in which she was at this time of year, through the loss of her foster-child. They, however, received the stranger as well as herself with the utmost kindness. The bride made the remark, when the stranger turned his back, that he was like Mac an Uidhir but when his face was towards her he appeared like a stranger.

whom she had never seen before; but that her heart warmed
towards him. The custom was then gone through of the
stranger drinking out of the bride's glass, and Mac-an-Uidhir
when doing this, slipped a _ring into the glass_, which, she
immediately recognised as that of her first lover. The whole
matter was then upset, and the party for whom the preparations
were made were dispersed, and the bride followed the fortunes
of her first lover.

Of a song made by the foster-mother to Mac-an-Uidhir,
when he was reported to have been drowned, and was looked
upon as dead, the following verses have been preserved. In
the translation the literal words are given, but no attempt is
made at reducing them to the rhyme which is essential in
English poetry.

> "Thou good son of Euar
>   Of generous and noble heart
> At one time little I thought
>   It would ever happen
> That you would be drowned
>   And your boat return empty
> While its irons would last
>   And repair was not needed
> While its stern-post stood,
>   Its sides and prow,
> While yards would hold out,
>   Or a fragment of its oak.
> Your well ordered new plaid
>   Is on the surface of the grey waves
> Your head is the sport of the little gull
>   And your side of the big gull;
> Your sister is without brother
>   And your mother without son
> Your bride without husband
>   And poor me without god-son."

Ach a dheagh Mhic an Uidhir
  'G an robh an cridhe fial farsuinn
Bha mi uair 's beag shaoil mi
  Gu 'm faodadh sid tachairt
Gu 'm biodh tus' air do bhàthadh
  'S do bhàta tighinn dachaidh
Fhad 's a mhaireadh a h-iaruinn
  'S nach iarradh i calcadh
    Thùg horoinn O.

Fhad 's a mhaireadh a h-iaruinn
  'S nach iarradh i calcadh
Fhad 's a mhaireadh a h-earluinn
  Agus tàthadh 's a saidhean
Fhad 's a mhaireadh a slatan
  Agus bloidhean d'a darach
    Thùg horoinn O.

Fhad 's a mhaireadh a slatan
  'S bloidhean d'a darach :
Tha do bhreacan ùr uallach
  Air uachdar nan glas thonn
'S fuil do chinn aig an fhaoilinn
  'S fuil do thaobh aig an fharspaig
    Thùg horoinn O.

'S fuil do chinn aig an fhaoilinn
  'S fhuil do thaobh aig an fharspaig :
Tha do phiuthar gun bhràthair
  'S do mhàthair gun mhac dheth
Do bhean òg 's i gun chéile
  'S truagh mi fhéin dheth gun dalta.
    Thùg horoinn O.

There is quite a modern instance, perhaps about the beginning of this century, of a native of the islet of Ulva, near Mull, having been driven during a snowstorm to *Heisgeir-nan-Cuiseag* (High Rock of Windlestraws) and passing the winter there alone till he was taken off early in the following summer. He, too, must have subsisted on whelks and what he could get along the shore. He was going home from Tiree.

Anxious to be at home at the New-year O.S., he, with a companion, left Tiree, and before going far a snowstorm came on, and the wind increased in violence till they were driven they did not know where. The companion got benumbed and died in the boat. It could only be said by the survivor that they passed very high rocks on some island.

The boat was cast ashore on Heisker, and the poor man left in it had to pass the winter as best he could, without food or shelter.

The islet is too distant from Canna for him to have been observed by any signal he could make.

STEEPING THE WITHIES.

THERE is an expression in Gaelic "It is time to steep the withies" ("*Tha 'n t-àm bhi bogadh nan gad*"), meaning, it is time for one to leave or make his escape from the company he is in. This expression is said to have arisen in this way. A little undersized man and good archer was sitting on a stool by his own fireside, when enemies intent on securing his person came in to the house. He sat quietly, but his wife going backwards and forwards through the house, and being ready-witted, when she understood the character of the intruders, gave a slap on the ear to her husband saying, as if he were merely the herd boy, "It is time to steep the withies" ("*Tha 'n t-àm bhi bogadh nan gad*"). He immediately left the house, and she managed to put his bow and arrows out at the window. He having stationed himself in a favourable locality did not allow a single one of his enemies to leave the house without killing them with his arrows, one by one as they came out at the door. Regarding the truth of this story it is noticeable, that uniformly throughout the Highlands the expression, "It is time to steep the withies" ("*Tha 'n t-àm bhi bogadh nan gad*"), means, not that it is time to prepare for action, but that it is time for one to make himself scarce. A story of the same kind is told of King Alfred the Great, that he escaped from his enemies in somewhat the same way. In olden times the harnessing of animals for carrying burdens, ploughing, etc., was done by means of withies made of willow, sea-bent,* or other accessible material, iron being scarce and difficult to procure, and these withies had to be steeped before work with them was commenced. It

---

* Tough Grass growing by the shore.

required a good deal of acquaintance with the work before the horse was fully equipped with pack-saddle, creels, and other equipments for which withies were necessary, and the only means available. The names of some of these withies still survive *e. g.* the *Gad-tarraich* is the Gaelic name still in use, although the material is leather, and not withies, to denote a belly-band.

LITTLE JOHN OF THE WHITE BAG.

(IAIN BEAG A' BHUILG BHAIN).

THIS doughty little archer was attached to the family of the MacLachlans of *Coruanain,* or little Lamb-dell, near Fort-William, on the borders of Inverness-shire and Argyleshire. He derived his name from his carrying a white bag of arrows, which he was very skilful in the use of. In far off and unsettled times, when a foray or *creach* was being taken from *Coruanain,* one of the raiders, having met little John, said, "Little John of the White Bag, I will mount the hill side quicker than you" *(Iain bhig a' Bhuilg Bhàin, bheir mise am fireach dhiot).* In a struggle it is always an advantage, even when other things are even, to have the higher position on a hill side. Little John replied, "The hand of your father and grandfather be over you, White Stirk, I will put the Brankes (or Iron Gag) on you *("Làmh d' athair 's do sheanair ort, a Ghamhain Bhàin cuiridh mise biorach ort").* The *biorach,* branker, was a spiked iron gag, or instrument set with pointed iron pins, fixed round the head of calves to keep them from sucking. The expression "The hand, &c., be over you" was a common expression, meaning much the same as the English "Look out," or "Take care of yourself." Saying this, Little John let fly an arrow which struck the other in the forehead, toppled him over, and put an end to the discussion.

THE KILLING OF BIG ANGUS OF ARDNAMURCHAN.

(Aonghas Mor Mac'Ill'-Eoin), Big Angus, Son of John, At Cor-Ospuinn in Morven.

In Ardnamurchan, where the district of Kintra commences, there is a streamlet that falls into Loch-Moidart, which lies along the north of Ardnamurchan, called *Faoghail Dhòmhnuill Chonalaich.* This streamlet derives its name from Donald MacDonald, or MacConnell, having been slain there under the following circumstances. Tradition is uniform as to the incident which gave its name to the place, and as to the circumstances under which the murder was committed. Donald was the heir to the chieftainship of Ardnamurchan, but his uncle, Big Angus, wishing to secure the estate for himself, waylaid his nephew at the ford mentioned, which is very difficult to jump across when the tide is in, as he was on his way to be married to a daughter of the then Chief of Lochiel. While Donald was jumping across the ford, one of Big Angus's men shot an arrow in his face, so that when he touched the ground on the other side, he staggered and reeled. Before he fell prostrate Big Angus said that he would wonder if his nephew would dance as merrily at his marriage with the daughter of the One-eyed Chief of meat-broth *(saoil an dannsadh tu co cridheil sin air banais nighean Cham-na-eanraich)*. The meaning of this nick-name given to the Chief of Lochiel is a covert allusion to the cattle-lifting of Lochiel. Before the introduction of tea, extract of meat was largely made use of, and even meal was mixed with it for those in strong health, but weak, and even chicken broth, was given to those who were in delicate health. Some say that the Chief referred to was *Ailein nan Creach* (Allan the Cattle-lifter), who derived his name from the number of cattle-spoils that he lifted. Lochaber being a wild and remote district was not unnaturally a place to which cattle forays were taken when people sought "the beeves that made the broth" in other localities.

In Gregory's History of the Western Islands *Dòmhnull Conalach* is called John, probably from the Chiefs of Ardnamurchan being known as Mac-'ic-Iain, the son of the son of John, and mention is made of his murder. Several families who have in recent times come to Coll from Ardnamurchan call themselves Johnstones.

Big Angus himself had a house near Strontian strongly fortified according to the ideas of those days. It was surrounded by a deep ditch *(Tigh daingean dige)* and what is now called a moated Grange. On hearing that Lochiel with a strong band of followers was on his way to avenge the death of the young Chief of Ardnamurchan, Big Angus fled, but he was closely pursued by the avengers. Having come to Cor-ospuinn in Morven he looked behind him, when the sun was rising, to see if his pursuers were coming. Lifting his helmet and shading his eyes with his hand when looking intently sunwards, one of the pursuers, a little man, remarked, "Would not this be a good opportunity for killing him?" Another answered, "It is not your trifling hand that would slay the powerful man." *(Cha 'n i do làmh leibideach a leagadh an duine foghainteach).* The little man replied, "Would not an arrow do it" *(Nach deanadh saighead e),* saying this, he launched an arrow which struck Big Angus in the forehead and killed him.

NOTE.

BIG ANGUS OF ARDNAMURCHAN.

(Aonghas mòr Mac 'ic Eoin)

The incidents of this story occurred about 1596. The house of the redoubtable Angus was at *Ath na h-éilde* (Ford of the Hind (deer), opposite *Druim-nan-torran* (The Ridge of Knolls), near *Sròn an t-slthean,* Strontian, the Promontory of the Fairy Dwelling. He had a bad wife, who was continually urging him to make himself Chief of the clan, and it was at her instigation that he waylaid his nephew at Kintra. On hearing that the Chief was to be married to the daughter of Lochiel, his wife warned big Angus that he would yet be reduced to draw the peat creels *(tarruing nan cliabh mòine)* for his nephew. Angus was the first to be at Kintra, at the river, and the first to cross. The guests were assembled at Lochiel for the marriage of Donald MacDonald, when word was brought of his having been slain. Immediately the assembled guests with their followers set off to take vengeance, and, finding Big Angus's house deserted, they tied tinder *(spong*)* to an arrow and set the moated house on fire. The place where Angus was slain in Morven is still called *Leac na Saighead* (The Ledge of the Arrow), and the archer was *Iain Dubh Beag Innse-ruith* (Little Black John of Inch-rui). Big Dugald Mac-Donald *(Dughal mòr MacRaonuil),* of Morar had his hand similarly fastened by an arrow to his forehead.

---

* Amadon—made from a fungus. A.C.

THE LAST CATTLE RAID IN TIREE.

It seems to have been a kind of raid or robbery to which the island of Tiree was particularly liable. Plunderers and pirates, having chosen a suitable day when the seas about the island were at rest, and the cattle could be easily got on board the galley, or *birlinn*, carried on depredations far and wide on the island. Once the cattle were got by them on board the galley, they looked upon themselves as safe from pursuit.

There are two traditions in existence of the island having been so visited, and their fate will illustrate the manner in which, in unsettled times, such expeditions were conducted. The last foray of the kind was not successful, but the cattle and sheep were collected for taking away. The people got warning in time, and the cattle-lifters had to make their escape, leaving their booty behind them.

The last successful foray was in the days of the Tanister of Torloisk, and seems to have been only sometime previous to or about the '45. The account which tradition gives of it is that the Tanister, or second heir *(proximus haeres)*, of Torloisk in Mull was called Malise MacLean. His first name is somewhat peculiar, and not common among the MacLeans or any other West Highland clan, and was given to him in this manner. The heir of Torloisk was a promising healthy boy, but the succeeding children of the then chief were dying young. The Chief was then advised by the sages of his race to give to his child the name of the first person whom he met on the way to have the child baptized. The first person encountered was a poor beggar man who had the name of Malise. A name given in this way was known as *ainm rathaid*, or road name, and was deemed as proof against evil. The father gave this name to the child who survived and became Tanister. Being without the prospect of an estate the Tanister thought he would come to Tiree, and piece by piece get an estate for himself. He came to have the half, third, or other share of the town-ship of *Baile-meadhonach*, now called Middleton, in Tiree, and married, and his descendants are still known.

One day, a galley, with sixteen men on board *(Bìrlinn 's sea fir dheug)*, came to Soraba beach. The men landed and collected every live animal that was about the place. At the time, the Tanister happened to be fishing at the rocks in Kenavara Hill, and on coming home soon after and hearing what had been done, he called to his neighbours asking them what they meant to do, were they going with him to turn the raid *(creach)*. They all refused for fear of being killed, as the freebooters were a strong party. He said, " I will not do that ; I prefer to fall in the attempt *(tuiteam 's an oidhirp)*, rather than let my cattle be taken." He took with him his sword and followed the spoilers. When he came to the end of the pathway and within sight of the galley, he stood before the creach. The freebooters told him to leave the road or he would feel the consequences *(Gu'm biodh a' bhuil dha)*. He answered, "I will not leave, and the consequences will be to you, until I get my own." He got this as he seemed determined, and when he had got it, he asked also the cow of a poor woman from the same township as himself, and having got this also, he said they might do with the rest what they liked. The plan of the robbers was to drive the cattle to the beach, where the galley was, and throwing them down and tying their forelegs together *(ceangal nan ceithir chaoil)*, place them on bearers, or planks, and put them in the boat. When they had done so, they made off, and no one knew whence they had come or whither they went. This was the last succesful raid of the kind raised in Tiree.

Subsequent to this creach, and in the time of Mr. Charles Campbell being Minister of Tiree, several galleys, or *bìrlinnean,* each with its complement of men, and in addition each with a pretending minister and his man, made their appearance on the coast of Tiree. In those days every minister took his man along with him, and in this case each minister but one took his man from the boat. Wandering open-air preachers were in those times called hillock ministers *(ministearan nan cnoc)*, and the one to whom the story refers was to officiate at *Ceathramh Mhurdat*, or Fourth Part, called Murdat, now embraced in the farm of Hough,* and which was then thickly populated. Having sent due intimation round of his service, most of the people were drawn to hear him. His man was left behind to give him warning of any disturbance of the expedition which might occur. After he had been speaking for some time his man came in. The islanders had become aware of the nature of the invasion. The sheep and the horses were gathered at the back of the hill of Hough, and a band of the cattle-lifters had surrounded them for to drive them to the shore. A number who had not got to the preaching had observed this, and following them, took the sheep and horses from them. Immediately, the minister's man ran with all possible speed to warn the preacher at Murdat. When he came to where the sermon was, the preacher concluded, and handing the book to his man, venturing to think that the people would not understand him, said, as if reading a line, " MacLellan, beloved friend, where did you leave the *Shockum sho* ? "—*i.e.,* the booty. *(Mhac-'ill-fhaolain, a dhuine ghaolaich, c' àite an d' fhàg thu an 'seogam seoth' ?).* The incomer taking the book, and as if intoning the psalm, said, " Matters are worse than we thought ; they have taken from us the plaintive bleaters " *('s miosa tha na mar a shaoil : thug iad uainn an 'cirri-mèh'): cirri-mèh* is but an imitation of the bleating of sheep, and is found used in different localities as a pet or ludicrous name for sheep.

* Pronounced Hoch.

The people sang along with the precentor. They did not
know but that the words may have been part of the psalm,
when one who was smarter and more ready-witted than the
rest got up and said, "We have been long enough here, these
men are robbers, and not ministers." The service was concluded, the people going to look after their cattle, and the
minister and his man making their way with all speed to where
the galleys lay. Before the people could overtake them, they
got on board and made off, leaving their booty behind, and
glad to escape with their lives.

LOCHBUIE'S TWO HERDSMEN.

THIS tale was written down as it was told by Donald Cameron,
Rùdhaig, Tiree, more than twenty-five years ago, and to whose
happy and retentive gift of memory it is a pleasure to recur.
He had a most extensive stock of old lore, and along with it
much readiness and willingness to communicate what he knew.
In this the ludicrous element is natural, and the events seem to
follow each other as a matter of course, so that the tale, so far
as probability is concerned, may be true enough. It is one of
the few tales to which a date is attached, and so far as history
can be consulted the state of the country at that time makes
it probable enough. Loch Buie is a district lying to the South
of the Island of Mull, pleasantly situated. The tale runs as
follows :—

In 1602 Lochbuie had two herdsmen, and the wife of one herdsman went to the house of the other herdsman. The housewife was in before her, and had a pot on the fire. "What have you in the pot?" said the one who came in. " Well there it is," she said, "a drop of *brochan* which the goodman will have with his dinner."

" What kind of *brochan* is it ?" said the one who came in.

" It is *dubh-bhrochan*," (see note 1) said the one who was in.

" Isn't he, said she, "a poor man! Are you not giving him anything but that? I have been for so long a time under the Laird of Loch Buie, and I have not drank *brochan* without a grain of beef or something in it. Don't you think it is but a small thing for the Laird of Loch Buie though we should get an ox every year. Little he would miss it. I will send over my husband to-night, and you will bring home one of the oxen."

When night came she sent him over. The wife then sent the other away. The one said, " you will steal the ox from the fold, and you will bring it to me, and we will be free ; I will swear that I did not take it from the fold, and you will swear that you did not take it home."

The two herdsmen went away. In those days they hanged a man, when he did harm, without waiting for law or sentence, and at this time Lochbuie had hanged a man in the wood. The herdsmen went and kindled a fire near a tree in the wood as a signal to the one who went to steal. One sat at the fire, and the other went to steal the ox.

The same night a number of gentlemen were in the mansion (2) at Loch Buie. They began laying wagers with Lochbuie that there was not one in the house who would take the shoe off the man who had been hanged that day. Lochbuie laid a wager that there was. He called up his big lad MacFadyen (see note 3), and said to him was he going to let the wager go against him. The big lad asked what the wager was about. He said to him that they were maintaining that there was no one in his

c

court who could take the shoe off the one who had been hanged that day. MacFadyen said he would take off him the shoe and bring it to them where they were.

MacFadyen went on his way. When he reached, he looked and saw the man who had been hanged warming himself at a fire. He did not go farther on, but returned in haste. When he came they asked him if he had the shoe. He told them he had not, for that yon one was with a withy basket of peats before him, warming himself. "We knew ourselves," said the gentlemen, "that you had only cowards."

The lameter, who was over, said, "It is a wrong thing you are doing in allowing him to lose the wager. If I had the use of my feet, I would go and take his leg off as well as his shoe before I would let Lochbuie lose the wager."

"Come you here," said the big lad, "and I will put a pair of feet that you never had the like of under you." He put the lameter round his neck (lit. the bone of his neck), and off he went. When they came in sight of the man who was warming himself the lameter sought to return. MacFadyen said they would not return. They went nearer to the man who was warming himself. The one that was at the fire lifted his head and observed them coming. He thought it was his own companion, the one who had gone to steal the ox, who was come. He spoke and said, "Have you come?" "I have," said MacFadyen. "And have you got it?" "Yes," said Mac-Fadyen. "And is it fat?"

"Whether he is fat or lean, there he is to you," and he threw the lameter on to the fire.

MacFadyen took to his heels (lit. put on soles) and fled as fast as ever he did. Off went the lameter after him. He put the four oars on for making his escape. The one at the fire rose, thinking there were some who had come to pry upon himself, and that he was now caught. He went after the lameter to make his excuses to the Laird of Loch Buie. The lameter was observing him coming after him, feeling quite sure that it was the one who had been hanged.

MacFadyen reached, and they asked him if he had taken the shoe off the man. He said they did not ; that he asked him if the lameter was fat, and that he was sure he had him eaten up

home. He went away with him and never got the like, going through hill, and through mud and dirt, till he came to the house of the other woman. He knocked at the door. The wife rose and let him in.

" How have things happened with you ?" " Never you mind, whatever ; but, alas ! he has been hanged since we went away."

The wife took to roaring and crying.

Do not say a word," he said, " or else you and I will be

court who could take the shoe off the one who had been hanged
that day. MacFadyen said he would take off him the shoe and
bring it to them where they were.

MacFadyen went on his way. When he reached, he looked
and saw the man who had been hanged warming himself at a
fire. He did not go farther on, but returned in haste. Wh.

The translation of lines 6 and 7 renders the Gaelic idiom
exactly. Translated more freely into English it would run,
"and the lameter came, and with yon terrified cry demanded
admittance, saying that the hanged man was coming after him."

the lameter on to the fire.

MacFadyen took to his heels (lit. put on soles) and fled as
fast as ever he did. Off went the lameter after him. He put
the four oars on for making his escape. The one at the fire
rose, thinking there were some who had come to pry upon
himself, and that he was now caught. He went after the
lameter to make his excuses to the Laird of Loch Buie. The

lameter was observing him coming after him, feeling quite sure that it was the one who had been hanged.

MacFadyen reached, and they asked him if he had taken the shoe off the man. He said they did not ; that he asked him if the lameter was fat, and that he was sure he had him eaten up before now. The lameter came, and that cry in his head for to let him in, for that yon one was coming. He was let in. The moment this was done, the one who had been on the gallows knocked at the door, to let him in. Lochbuie said he would not.

" I am your own herdsman." They now let him in. He then began to tell how he and the other herdsman went to steal the ox, and that he thought it was the other herdsman who had returned, and it was that made him ask if he was fat. Lochbuie and his guests had much sport and merriment over this all night. They kept the herdsman till it was late on in the night telling them how it happened to him.

The one who went to steal the ox now came back and reached the tree where he left the other herdsman, but found no one. He began to search up and down, and became aware of the one dangling from the tree.

" Oh," said he, " you have been hanged since I went away, and I will be to-morrow in the same plight that you are in. It has been an ill-guided object, and the tempting of women that sent us on the journey."

He then went over and took the man off the tree to take him home. He went away with him and never got the like, going through hill, and through mud and dirt, till he came to the house of the other woman. He knocked at the door. The wife rose and let him in.

" How have things happened with you ?" " Never you mind, whatever ; but, alas ! he has been hanged since we went away."

The wife took to roaring and crying.

Do not say a word," he said, " or else you and I will be

hanged to-morrow. We will bury him in the garden, and no one will ever know about it. "And now," he said, "I will be returning to my own house."

The one that was in Loch Buie thought it was time for him now to go home. He knocked at his own door. His wife did not say a word. He then called out to be let in.

"I will not," said the wife, "for you have been hanged, and you will never get in here."

"I have not yet been hanged," he said.

"Be that as it may to you," she said, "you will never come here."

The advice he gave himself was to go to the house of the other herdsman. He called out at that one's door to let him in.

"You will not come in here. I got enough carrying you home on my back, and you after being hanged."

There was a large window at the end of the house. He went in at the window. "Get up," he said, "and get a light, and you will see that I have not been hanged any more than yourself." When he saw who he had, he kept him till morning, till day came. They then talked together, telling each other what had happened to them on both sides, and thought they would go to Lochbuie, and tell him all that occurred to them. When Lochbuie heard their story, there was not a year after that but he gave each of them an ox and a boll of meal.

LOCHABUIDHE 'S A DHA BHUACHAILLE.

ANN an 1602 bha dà bhuachaille aig Lochabuidhe, 's thàinig
bean an darna buachaille gu tigh a' bhuachaille eile ; agus bean-
an-tighe stigh roimpe 's poit aice air teine; " Dé th' agaibh anns
a' phòit?" ars' an té a thàinig a stigh. " Ma ta," ars' ise, " deur
de bhrochan a bhios aig an duine le 'dhìnneir," " 'Dé," ars' an
té a thàinig a stigh, " an seòrsa brochain a th' ann?" " Tha,"
ars' an té a bha stigh, " dubh-bhrochan."[1] " Nach esan," ars'
ise, " an duine truagh? Nach 'eil thu 'toirt da dad ach sin?
Tha mise an uiread so de ùine fuidh thighearna Lochabuidhe,
's cha d' òl mi brochan gun fhionnan-feòla no rud-eiginn ann.
Saoil nach beag do thighearna Lochabuidhe, ged a gheibhea-
maide damh 's a' bhliadhna ; nach beag a dh' ionndrainneadh e
e? Cuiridh mise an duine agam fhéin a nall an nochd 's bheir
sibh dhachaigh fear de na daimh."

'N uair thàinig an oidhche chuir i nall e. Chuir a' bhean an
so air falbh an duin' eile. Thuirt an darna fear, " Goididh tusa
an damh thar na buaile, 's bheir thu thugamsa e, agus bithidh
sinn saor ; mionnaichidh mise nach d' thug mi thar na buaile e,
's mionnaichidh tusa nach d' thug thu dhachaigh e."

Dh' fhalbh an dà bhuachaille. 'S an àm sin chrochadh iad
duine tra 'dheanadh e cron, gun fheitheamh ri lagh no binn ;
ach anns na lathan bha tighearna Lochabuidhe an déigh duine
'chrochadh stigh 's a' choille. Dh' fhalbh iadsan 's dh' fhadaidh
iad teine aig craoibh 's a' choille, mar chomharradh do 'n fhear
a chaidh a ghoid. Shuidh fear aig an teine 's chaidh am fear
eile a ghoid an daimh. Air an oidhche fhéin bha mòran de
dhaoin'-uaisle 's a' Mheigh[2] aig tighearna Lochabuidhe. Bhuail
iad air cur gheall ri tighearna Lochabuidhe nach robh duine 's

an tigh aige a bheireadh a' bhròg thar an fhir a chaidh chrochadh an diugh.   Chuir tighearna Lochabuidhe geall riù-san gu 'n robh. Ghlaodh e nuas air a ghille mhòr Mac Phaidean.[3] Thuirt e ris an robh e brath an geall a leigeadh air.   Dh' fharraid an gille mòr c' ar son a bha 'n geall.   Thuirt e ris, gu 'n robh iad ag ràdh nach robh duine 'n a chùirt a bheireadh a' bhròg thar an fhir a chaidh chrochadh an diugh.   Thuirt Mac Phaidean gu 'n tugadh esan dheth a' bhròg 's gu 'n tugadh e thuga ann an sud i.

Dh' fhalbh Mac Phaidean air a thurus. 'Nuair a ràinig e sheall e 's chunnaic e 'm fear a chaidh chrochadh 'deanamh a gharaidh.   Cha deach e na b' fhaid' air aghaidh, 's thill e le cabhaig. 'Nuair a ràinig e thuirt iad ris, an robh a' bhròg aige. Thuirt e riu nach robh, gur h-ann a bha 'm fear ud 's làn cléibh de mhòine air a bhialthaobh 's e 'deanamh a gharaidh.   "Dh' aithnich sinn-fhéin," ars' na daoin'-uaisle, "nach robh agad ach an gealtair."   Thuirt an clàraineach[4] a bha thall, "Is ceàrr an rud a tha thu 'deanamh, an geall a leigeadh air ; na 'm biodh comas nan cas agam-fhéin dh' fhalbhainn 's bheirinn a' chas dheth co math ris a' bhròig mu 'n leiginn an geall air tighearna Lochabuidhe !"

"Thig thusa so," ars' an gille mòr, "'s cuiridh mise dà chois nach deachaidh riamh 'n leithid ortsa fothad."   Chuir e 'n clàraineach mu chnàimh 'amhaich, 's dh' fhalbh e leis. 'Nuair thainig iad 'an sealladh an duine a bha 'deanamh a gharaidh, dh' iarr an clàraineach tilleadh.   Thuirt Mac Phaidean nach tilleadh. Dhlùthaich iad ris an fhear a bha 'deanamh a gharaidh.   Thog am fear a bha aig an teine a cheann, 's mhothaich e dhoibh-san a' tighinn.   Shaoil leis gur h-e a chompanach fhéin, am fear a chaidh a ghoid an daimh, a bha air tighinn.   Labhair e 's thuirt e, "An d' thàinig tu ?"   "Thàinig," ars' Mac Phaidean. "'S am bheil e agad ?"   "Tha," ars' Mac Phaidean.   "'S am bheil e reamhar ?"   "Biodh e reamhar no caol agad, sin agad e !" 's e a' tilgeadh a' chlàraineich mu 'n teine.

Chuir Mac Phaidean na buinn air, 's theich e co làidir 's a rinn e riamh. Leum an clàraineach air falbh as a dhéighinn, chuir e na ceithir raimh⁵ orra gu teicheadh. Dh' éirich am fear a bh' aig an teine, agus dùil aige gur h-e feadhainn a thainig a dh' fharcluais air fhéin a bh' ann, 's gu 'n robh e nis a sàs. Dh' fhalbh e as déighinn a' chlàraineach, dhol a ghabhail a leithsgeul do thighearna Lochabuidhe. Bha an clàraineach 'g a fhaicinn a' tighinn as a dhéighinn, 's e làn-chinnteach gur h-e 'm fear a chaidh chrochadh a bh' ann.

Ràinig Mac Phaidean. Dh' fharraid iad dheth an d' thug iad bròg bharr an duine. Thuirt e nach d' thug, gu 'n dubhairt e ris-san an robh an clàraineach reamhar, 's gu 'n robh e cinnt-each gu 'n robh e air 'itheadh aca roimhe so.

Ràinig an clàraineach 's an glaodh ud 'n a cheann, esan a leigeadh a stigh, gu 'n robh am fear ud a' tighinn. Leigeadh a stigh e. Am buileach a bha e stigh, bhuail am fear a bh' air a' chroich 's an dorus, esan a leigeadh a stigh. Thuirt fear Lochabuidhe nach leigeadh. "Is ann a th' annam," ars' esan, "am buachaille agaibh fhéin." Leig iad 'an so a stigh e. Bhuail e so air innseadh dhoibh mar chaidh e-fhéin 's am buachaille eile a ghoid an daimh; gu 'n do shaoil esan gur h-e 'm buachaille eile a bha air tilleadh leis an damh, gur h-e 'thug air a dh' fheòraich an robh e reamhar. Bha spòrs is fearas-chuid-eachd anabarrach aig tighearna Lochabuidhe 's aig 'uaislean air a so fad na h-oidhche. Chum iad aca am buachaille gus an robh e ro-fhada dh' oidhche 'g innseadh naigheachd mar a dh' éirich dha.

Thàinig so am fear a chaidh a ghoid an daimh. Ràinig e 'chraobh aig an d' fhàg e 'm buachaille eile 's cha d' fhuair e duine. Bhuail e air siubhal sìos 's suas; mhothaich e 'n slaod ud nuas ris a' chraoibh. "O," ars' esan, "tha thusa air do chrochadh bho 'n a dh' fhalbh mise, 's bithidh mise am maireach air an ruith air am bheil thu fhéin. 'S e an turus mi-shealbhach, 's buaireadh nam ban, a chuir sinne air an turus,"

Ghabh e null 's thug e' n duine bhàrr na croiche g' a thoirt dachaigh. Dh' fhalbh e 's cha d' fhuair e leithid dol roimh mhonadh 's roimh pholl 's roimh eabar riamh; mu dheireadh ràinig e tigh na mnatha bha 'n duine air a chrochadh aice. Bhuail e 's an dorus; dh' éirich a' bhean 's leig i stigh e. " Ciamar a dh' éirich dhuibh ? " ars' a' bhean. " Is coma leatsa co-dhiù, mo thruaighe ! tha e air a chrochadh o 'n a dh' fhalbh sinn."

Chaidh a' bhean gu glaodhaich agus gu caoineadh. " Na abair guth," ars' esan, " air neo bithidh tu fhéin 's mise air ar crochadh am màireach. Tiodhlaicidh sinn anns a' ghàradh e, 's cha bhi fios aig duine am feasd air. Nis (ars' esan), bithidh mise falbh dhachaigh thun mo thighe féin."

Ach smaointich am fear a bha 'n Lochbuidhe gu 'n robh an t-àm aige tighinn dachaigh nis. Bhuail e 's an dorus aige fhéin. Cha dubhairt a bhean guth. Ghlaodh e so a leigeadh a stigh. " Cha leig," ars' a bhean, " 's ann a tha thu air do chrochadh ; cha tig thu so am feasd !"

" Cha 'n 'eil mi air mo chrochadh fhathast," thuirt esan.

" Biodh sin mar a dh' fheudas e dhuit," ars' ise, " cha 'n fhaigh thu stigh so am feasd."

Is e 'chomhairle a smaointich e air, dol gu tigh a' bhuach-aille eile. Ghlaodh e 's an dorus aig an fhear ud, a leigeil a stigh. Thuirt am fear ud, " Cha tig thu stigh an so ; fhuair mise gu leòir 'g ad thoirt dachaigh air mo mhuin 's tu air do chrochadh." Bha uinneag mhòr air ceann an tighe 's ghabh e dh' ionnsuidh na h-uinneig. Thàinig e stigh air an uinneig. " Eirich," ars' esan, " 's las solus 's gu 'm faic thu nach do chrochadh mise na 's mò na 'chrochadh tu-fhéin."

'Nuair chunnaic e gur e a bh' aige, chum e aige e gu maduinn, gus an d' thàinig an latha. Chuir iad an so an guth ri chéile a dh' innseadh dhaibh mar a dh' éirich dhaibh thall 's a bhos; gu 'n rachadh iad gu tighearna Lochabuidhe 's gu 'n innseadh iad dha na h-uile dad mar a dh' éirich dhaibh. 'Nuair chuala tighearna Lochabuidhe mar a dh' éirich doibh, cha robh bliadhna tuilleadh nach tugadh e damh do na h-uile fear dhiubh, 's bolla mine.

NOTES.

1.—*Dubh-bhrochan* is a thin mixture of oatmeal and water, without meat or vegetables. This seems to have been a popular drink in olden times. When the Lord of the Isles kept state at Duntulm Castle in Skye, no one was admitted into the potentate's body-guard unless he could take the vessel (diorcal), containing the liquid, with one hand from his companion, take his own mouthful, and pass it on to the next. In the Island of Mull, adjoining the Sound, and opposite Ardtornish, once the seat of the Lords of the Isles, there is a place, probably deriving its name from some fancied resemblance to this dish, called Loch Diorcal.

2.—Moy Castle is situated near the modern mansion-house of Lochbuie, and the reference appears to be to it in the Gaelic text. (Ed.)

3.—MacFadyens were said by one of the clan, of whose judgment and intelligence the writer has cause to think very highly, to have been the first possessors of Lochbuie, and when expelled, that they became a race of wandering artificers, (*Sliochd nan òr-cheard*—the race of goldsmiths), in *Beinn-an-aoinidh* and other suitable localities in Mull. The race is a very ancient one, but it has often been noticed that they are without a chief.

4.—*Clàraineach* means one on boards. A person losing the use of his limbs, and going on all fours, with boards or pieces of wood below his hands and knees, and with which he could more easily drag himself over the ground. When placed sitting, he could not move. In olden times the defects of humanity, which are now relieved by many means, were left entirely to chance or very simple aids, and were the objects of malevolent persecution, rather than of charitable or kindly consideration.

5.—*Na ceithir ràimh* (the four oars)—fled upon all fours. (Ed.)

MAC NEIL OF BARRA, AND THE LOCHLINNERS.

THE Lochlinners came to Barra at one time and they put Mac Neil to flight. He escaped to Ireland, where he remained. When his sons grew up, they heard themselves continually twitted as strangers, and called "Barraich." They resolved to find out the reason of this treatment, and one day, while at dinner, they demanded from their father an explanation of their being called by such an uncommon name as "Barraich" (Barraidhich); but he replied that the mention of that name caused him the deepest sorrow, and forbade them ever to mention it in his hearing again. "We will never eat a bite nor drink a drink again," they said, "till we know what the word means." He then explained the name and told them all that happened to him and how he had to suffer indignity and scorn as long as his powerful enemies the Norsemen held his lands. His sons on hearing the cause of their father's banishment resolved to try every means in their power to recover their inheritance. They began to fit out a galley *(bìrlinn)*, and when it was completed with masts, sails, oars, crew and compass, and in readiness to go away, their father gave them the point to Barra Head, and said, that if the man he left at Barra was still there, and whose name was Macillcary (Mac 'ille-charaich), he would direct them straight to the place where they were to go to in search of their enemies. Thus it happened *('s ann mar sin a bhà).* They found the man and told him who they were and the purpose for which they came. He bade them steer for Castle Bay *(Bàigh-a'-chaisteil)* and a light on the right-hand-side as they entered. They reached the house where the light was, but could get no entrance. They climbed to the roof, and looking through an opening saw a poor old man who was weeping bitterly. They called to him that they were friends, and on admitting them he told them how that day he had been paying his rent to the Lochlinners and wanted a few marks of it, for this they threatened him that if he did not return with the balance of the rent, he would receive next day at noon a certain number of lashes. The Mac Neils then told their errand, and the old man joyfully showed them the most direct and secret way to the Castle, in which was a well of pure water whose source was unknown. They took the castle, and went on to Kinloch (Ceannloch), and cleared Vaslam as well. They then sent word to their father, who came with a band of followers to their help, and others, native born, whom he had formerly known, and on whose friendship he could rely, as soon as the tidings of his return reached them, joined his band. An unacknowledged son whom he had left, came among the rest to his assistance. This son, from the circumstance, was known as Mac-an-amhar-uis (the son of doubt). When he put forward his claim, Mac Neil replied, "If you are a son of mine, prove it by clearing Eilean Fiaradh, before morning, of my enemies." "Give me the means then," Mac-an-amharuis answered, "and I will not leave the blood of one of the race in any part or place (*'s cha'n fhàg mi fuil fineig dhiubh 'an àite na'n ionad)*." Mac Neil gave him his own sword, and that night while the Lochlinners, who had been carousing heavily, slept soundly, he made his way and got secretly in to the castle which stands on an inlet before Eoligarry castle, eight miles from Castle Bay, and killed the inmates where they lay. It is said that their bodies are still to be seen when a violent storm drifts the sand hither and thither over the fort *(tigh-dìon)* where they were slain. From that day Mac Neil had his own rights.

AT the time MacLean of Dowart was proprietor of Tiree, this man, *Fionnladh Guibhneach*, was living near a small bay, *Port-nan-long*, in Balemartin, on the south side of the island *(air an leige deas)*. There was no other joinersmith but himself, or rather, there was none to equal him in skill in the five islands *(anns na còig eileanan)*. Balemartin and Mannal were in those days one farm-holding, and there were few people in the township. The change-house *(tigh-òsd)* was at the stream-let Gedans *(amhuinn Ghoidean)*, between Island House, the proprietor's residence, and the shore. At this time, also, there was fosterhood *(comhaltas)* between MacLeod of Dunvegan and MacLean of Tiree, by which they were bound to give proof of friendship for each other at whatever cost or whenever there was occasion on either side, and MacLeod, being in need of Finlay Guivnac's service, came with his boat *(bìrlinn)* to Tiree for him. He landed at *Port-nan-long* (the creek of sailing ships), and on reaching Island House was heartily welcomed by MacLean. When he asked for Finlay, he was told that he had not been at Island House for some days, "and it is not a good day when I do not see him," MacLean said. MacLeod said he came to take Finlay with him for a year's service; that all care would be taken of him, and if no misfortune or mischance befell either of them, he himself would bring him home at the end of the year. When MacLean heard this he said they would go in search of Finlay. They went, and as they were crossing the common *(an clar macharach)*, between the house and the streamlet, they met Finlay, who, having recovered from the attack of ill-humour, was, as was usually his daily custom, on his way to Island House. MacLeod asked after his health, and if he was yet able to do as good work as ever. Finlay said that in place of getting weaker as he got older, he was daily gaining in strength and vigour *(neart 's tàbhachd)* ; he was more active in walking, and could see better than he had ever done. MacLeod said he was surprised to hear that, as in Skye people were failing in strength and activity as they became older, "and it is curious that it is different with you." Finlay said he knew he was better now at walking and was gaining his eyesight, as formerly he could jump over Sorabai stream, but now he walked to the ford to get across ; and when he was younger, if he saw a person, it was as one, but now it was as two and three. They took Finlay with them to the change-house. When pledging MacLean's health, MacLeod, as was customary, said, "Wishing to get my wish from you, MacLean " *(Mo shainnseal ort, 'Mhic-'illeathain).*

" You are welcome to have your wish freely gratified " *('S e beatha le sainnseal),* * MacLean replied. "My wish is that I may get Finlay with me," MacLeod said. In returning the compliment MacLean said, " My wish is that I may keep Finlay to myself." " But I do not ask to keep him always," MacLeod said. They then settled the wages, and agreed between them that Finlay should go to Dunvegan, on the west coast of Skye, for a year's work, and lest he should be kept longer than that time, MacLean was to go with him. When Finlay went home and told his wife about the journey he was to take, she said to him, " You are very foolish to go so far away, when MacLean is giving you a good livelihood." " I must go at anyrate, and you must come with me," he said, and told her how he was not to remain in Skye, and that MacLean himself was going with him to make sure he would not be kept there, and that she was to go with them. " How can I do that," she said, "when MacLean will not allow a woman in the same boat with him ?" " I will put you in a

---

* *Sainnseal* means the giving of a free gift, or handsel.

hogshead," he said, "and when we reach Dunvegan there will be feasting and enjoyment, and when the nobility of MacLeod (*maithibh Siol Leòid*) are gathered, you will come in among the company as a poor woman, and I will manage the rest in such a way as that you may perhaps earn more than myself." She consented to this, and he put her at night with sufficient provision in the boat. They reached Dunvegan safely (*le deadh shoirbheachadh*). Finlay's wife got away unnoticed from the boat, and waited at a house near till the festivities began. When the crew and those who came in the boat reached the castle, there was much rejoicing; an abundant feast was provided, and company gathered, and the usual customs when tables were spread and guests invited, were observed. Among those who came to the gathering was a dependent of good position, who, through some trifling cause, had lost the favour of MacLeod. Finlay observed that he kept aloof from the company, and having ascertained the cause, advised him to pledge MacLeod's health, and at the same time make his grievance known. He took the advice, and said,

> "Esteemed was I in MacLeod's house
> When justice sat in his land,
> And I am a forgotten son to-night
> At the time of drawing in to wine (drinking),
> But this to you, son of Dark John,
> Who came in to-day or yesterday,
> I am the son of a hero
> Who was here in the past,
> Though I cannot to-day
> Get the hill for my cattle."

> ("Bu mhùirneach mise 'an tigh Mhic Leòid
> 'Nuair shuidh a' chòir 'n a thìr,
> 'S mac dì-chuimhnicht' mi 'n nochd 'n a theach
> 'An àm tarruing a steach gu fìon,
> Ach sud ortsa, mhic Iain Duibh,
> A thàinig stigh an diugh no 'n dé,
> Mise mac suinn a bh' ann riamh
> Ged nach fhaigh mi 'n diugh an sliabh g' am spréidh.")

" Good youth," MacLean said, " go you to Mull and I will give you land *(fearann)* there." He said,

> " I was a hero's son last year,
> But I am a son of sorrow this year;
> If I am put under a ~~third weight~~,
> I will be a son of Mull next year."

> (" Bu mhac suinn mi an uiridh,
> Ach mac mulaid mi 'm bliadhna ;
> Ma chuireas iad orm tuille treise,
> 'S mac Muileach mi air an ath·bhliadhna.")

" MacLeod's own lands are not yet exhausted," MacLeod said, and he restored him to his former place and privileges, and he never had to go to Mull or anywhere else for land.

During this time Finlay kept looking for his wife's appearance, and ~~whenever~~ he saw her in the doorway he called out to her, " Poor woman ! what has brought you here ? It must be some pressing need that made you come among the nobles of the Clan Leod to-night. Tell your story, and sure am I they will one and all be willing to give you help, and that they will not let you away as empty-handed as you have come." She said she was a poor woman who was bringing herself through life honestly as she best could, with help from those who took notice of her poverty and gave her charity, and that she came to the nobles of the Clan Leod, as they were gathered at this time, to try if they would help her. " Let your countrymen do as they like," Finlay said, " I will give you a calving cow *(mart-laoigh)*." MacLean looked at him in astonishment, and it was no wonder, when he heard him give away the only cow the poor woman in Balemartin had to the northern wife *(do 'n chaillich thuathaich)*. Everyone of the nobles present gave her a similar gift, till she had the nine cows. When the company left, and MacLean had an opportunity of speaking to Finlay, he said to him, " What made you give the only cow you had to the northern wife ?" " Do you know who the wife is ?" Finlay said. " What do I care what wife she is or was," MacLean said. " It was just my own wife who was there and got all the cows, and you need not give her yours till you return home," Finlay said. " And how did you bring her here ?" MacLean asked. " Ods ! MacLean," he said, " just in the big hogshead at your feet in the galley." " No death will ever happen to you but to be hanged for your quirks " *(cha tig bàs ortsa 'm feasd ach do chrochadh le d' raoitean)*, MacLean said, and he advised him to send the cattle to Mull, till they could be ferried to Tiree. Finlay took the advice, and sent his wife and the cows to MacLean's place at Benmolach, on the north-west side of Mull, and she got them to Balemartin, where MacLean on his return home sent her his own gift.

Finlay began his work and went on diligently with it that he might be ready at the end of the year to return home, and MacLeod came frequently where he was, more to hear what he had to say than to see the progress he was making with his work. One day, happening to find him at his breakfast, and observing that Finlay began at the back with a shape of butter *(measgan-ìme)* that was set before him, MacLeod asked him when he had finished, why he did not begin at the front of it. " I took it just from back to front as was wont at MacLean's table, where the measures were round *(far nach biodh na measgain 'n am bloidhean)*." On another occasion MacLeod found him paring a remnant of cheese *(cùl càise)*, and asked him when he had learned to pare cheese. " Since I came to MacLeod's Castle," he said : " it was not the custom to put a remnant on the inviting, merry, bountiful table in Mac-Lean's house *(air bòrd fiughaireach, aighearach, fialaidh Mhic'illeathain)*."

When the year had expired, MacLean, as had been agreed on, went to bring Finlay home. He was cordially received by MacLeod and was enjoying, after his journey, the usual hospit-alities prepared for guests of his rank, when he heard the sound of Finlay's hammer : " My loss ! *(mo chreach!)*," he said, " I have

too long delayed going where Finlay is." When he reached
him, he said, "Excuse me, Finlay, I have been rather a long
time of coming where you are." "I know that, MacLean," he
said,

> "The object of my contempt is the small table
> Where meanness would be (found):
> The object of my praise was the well filled table
> Where proud heroes sat.
> You did not take in Finlay Guivnac
> Nor remember him till the last."

> ("B' e mo laochan am bòrd suaile
> Air am bitheadh na laoich mhcamnach:
> Cha d' thug thusa stigh do ghobhainn Guibhneach,
> 'S cha do chuimhnich thu e gu anmoch.")

MacLean then asked after his welfare during the year, and
said among other things, he would like to hear what were his
opinions of the women of the MacLeod country since his
coming among them. "Well, I will tell you that," Finlay said,

> "If all the women of the Clan MacLeod,
> Small and great, old and young,
> Were gathered in one body,
> It would be one right one I would make out of them."

> ("Ged bhiodh mnathan Sìol Leòid,
> Beag is mòr, sean 's crìon,
> Air an càradh 'an aona bhodhaig
> 'S e aona bhean chòir a dheanainn dhiubh.")

"They will not be well pleased with your words." "They
will be better pleased with my words than I have been with
their ways," Finlay said; "I see it is time to return to Tiree,"
MacLean said.

When Finlay went to get payment from MacLeod before
leaving, and as they were conversing together after settling between them, MacLeod said he would lay a wager that the peats of
Tiree would not burn so well as the peats of Skye. "What is

D

your opinion, Finlay?" MacLean asked; "Shall I accept the wager?" "Well, as a matter of indifference I will wager they will not burn as well as those of the White Moss in Tiree (*Leòra! cuiridh mise geall uach gabh iad co maith ri mòine Bhlàir-bhàin 'an Tireadh*)," Finlay said, and the wager was laid. "I will try another wager," MacLeod said, "that our dogs will thrash the MacLean dogs." This wager was also accepted, and MacLeod came to Tiree with them, bringing peats and dogs with him in the galley. On putting the wagers to the test, the Skye peat when kindled lighted brightly with a great flare, but was soon burnt out. MacLean then asked if they would try the Tiree kind now. As none had been brought by the servants, and as it had previously been agreed on between them, MacLean asked Finlay to go for them himself. Finlay said perhaps it would not be the best that he would bring in. He went out, and gathering an armful of peats took and steeped them one by one (*fòid an dèigh fòid*) in a cask of oil. When MacLeod saw them he said, "O man, how wet they are! (*O dhuine, nach iad a tha fliuch*)." "The wetter they are, the livelier they will burn (*mar a's fliuiche 's ann a's braise iad*)," Finlay replied, putting them on ; and when they took fire they nearly burned the house. "Did I not say they would burn better than those of Skye," Finlay said to MacLeod, "and you have lost the wager." "Undoubtedly I have," the other replied. Next day the dog fight (*tabaid chon*) was to be tried. Finlay rose early and gave his dogs the strongest "crowdie" (*fuarag, a mixture of milk and meal*), and though they were smaller when the fight began, MacLeod's dogs could not hold one bout with them. "It is surprising," MacLeod said, "when one of my dogs is as big as two of MacLean's dogs." "You need not be at all surprised," Finlay said, "those here are of the race of dogs that were in the land of the Fians (*so sìolachadh nan con a bh' aca 's an Fhéinn*), and no other kind need try their strength against them." "If you were in the land of the

Fians, you came back, and no one need lay a wager with MacLean so long as he has you with him." MacLeod bade them farewell and returned home *(Dh' fhàg e beannachd aca 's thill e dhachaidh).*

BIG DEWAR OF BALEMARTIN, TIREE.

HE was John MacLean, a native of Dowart in the island of Mull, who fled to Jura.* He is said to have been the first man from that island who settled in Tiree, and on that account was known as Dewar *(Diùrach)*†. He and his seven sons were alike powerful and strong men. They held the township of Balemartin (on the south side of Tiree), including Sorabi, where a burying ground is, and where there was at one time a chapel to which was attached the land of Sorabi garden. At this time the people in the island were paying rent or tax *(càs)*, but it was found impossible to make big John Dewar submit to pay the tax. The first time any attempt was made to compel him to pay it, he took with him his seven sons to Island-House, the proprietor's residence, and put them on the sward in front of the

---

* The cause of John Dewar's flight to Jura is said to have been occasioned by his having given information to MacLaine of Lochbuie which was injurious to MacLean of Dowart, in a dispute that occurred between them.

† Several of John Dewar's descendents are at the present day in Tiree. They are known as *na Diùraich*, one family who are descended from the elder of his sons being cottars in Balemartin.

house *(air dòirlinn an eilein)*, saying, "This is the payment I have brought you, and you may take it or leave it." Another attempt to enforce payment from him ended as told in the following account :—

One day when he and his sons were ploughing, two of the sons being at Sorabi, as there were few people in the neighbourhood, and his sons were at some distance from him, he had to go himself to the smithy to repair the ploughshare *(a ghlasadh an t-suic)*. It was the beginning of summer, and he left the horses in the plough, eating the wild mustard *(sgeallan)* in the field where he was ploughing, grass and other herbage being scant. While their father was away at the smithy, the sons who were at Sorabi, on taking a look seawards, observed a boat *(blrlinn)* coming in towards the shore. It kept its course for the small bay of boats *(port nan long)*, in Balemartin, and had on board a very strong man called "Dark John Campbell" *(Iain Dubh Caimbeul)*, who was sent to collect the tax from those in the island who were unwilling to pay it. He had an able crew with him in the boat. They landed, and when they reached the place where Dewar was ploughing, the first thing they did was to seize the horses in the plough *(na h-eich a bha 's an t-seisreach)*, to take them away in the boat as payment of the tax. When they were almost ready to be off, Dewar came in sight on his return from the smithy. On seeing the unwelcome strangers he quickened his steps to intercept them, and took hold of the horses to take them back. Campbell drew his sword, bidding him be off as fast as he could or he would put his head beside his feet. Dewar drew his own sword and said, "Come on and do all you are able." The fray began between them, and Dewar was driving Campbell, Inveraray, backwards until he put him in among the graves *(lic)* in the burying-ground, and it so happened that Campbell stumbled on MacLean's cross and fell backwards. Before he could raise himself Dewar got the upper hand of him. On seeing him fall, his men were certain that he must have been killed, and they went away with the horses to the boat and put off to sea. "Let me rise," Campbell said, "and I will give you my word that I will never come again on the same errand." "I will," Dewar said, "but give me your oath on that, that it will be as that *(gu 'm bi sin mar sin)*." Campbell gave his word, "and more than that," he said, "I will send you the value of the horses when I reach Inveraray." "You will now come with me to my house," Dewar said, "and you need not have fear or dread ; your house-quarters and welcome will not be worse than my own, till you can find a way of returning home. In the course of some days Campbell got away, and he never returned again to "bullyrag" or intimidate any one. On reaching Inveraray he was as good as his word. He sold the horses and sent the price to Dewar, who was never compelled to pay the tax.

THE BIG LAD OF DERVAIG.

CONTEMPORARY with John Dewar of Balemartin, Tiree, the Big Lad was living at Dervaig, Mull, with his father, Charles, son of Fair Neil of Dervaig. This lad, as he grew up to manhood, became noted for his great strength and prowess, as well as for his handsome person. At the same time he was reckless and foolish. Despising his father's reproofs and heedless of his counsel, advice or admonitions, he went on in his mad career

until at last he purloined money from him, with which he
bought a ship and went sailing away, none of his friends knew
whither.   After some years he returned home, broken-down in
appearance, empty-handed, and a complete " tatterdemalion,"
having wrecked his ship on the coast of Ireland, and lost all
the wealth he had accumulated to repay his father, who was
now dead. The grieve *(an t-aoirean)* had the land, and he went
where he was.   The grieve told him about his father's death,
and advised him to go to his father's brother, Donald, son of
fair Neil, who had Hynish, Tiree, at that time, and whatever
advice he would get from him, to follow it, and he (the grieve)
would give him clothing and means to take him there, on
condition of being repaid when he returned.   As there was no
other way open to him of redeeming his past errors, he agreed
to the grieve's conditions and went to Tiree to his uncle, by
whom he was coldly received.   " What business has brought
you, and where are you going when you have come here ?"
" To ask advice from yourself," he said.   " Good was the
advice your father had to give, and you did not take it ; what
I advise you to do is, to go and enlist in the Black Watch, and
that will keep you out of harm.   You will stay here to-night,
and I will give you money to-morrow morning to take you to
the regiment," his uncle said.   His uncle was married to a
daughter of MacLean, Laird of Coll.   Her husband did not
tell her of his nephew's arrival, as he was displeased at his
coming.   When the Big Lad was leaving the house next
morning, she saw him passing the window and asked who the
handsome-looking stranger was.   On being told, she made him
return to the house, gave him food, drink, and clothing, and
on parting, money to take him on his way.   He returned to
Dervaig, paid the ploughman his due, and went off to the wars.
At the first place he landed, said to be Greenock, a pressgang
was waiting to seize whoever they could get to suit the king's
service, and on seeing this likely man they instantly surrounded

him, to carry him off by force. He turned about and asked what they wanted with him. They said, " To take you with us in spite of you." When he understood their intentions he opened his arms to their widest extent and drove all those before him, eighteen men, backwards into the sea, and left them there floating to get out the best way they could. He then made his way till he enlisted in the Black Watch, then on the eve of leaving for America, where it remained for seven years. During that time the Big Lad *(an Gille mòr)* won the esteem and commendation of his superiors in rank, by his exemplary conduct and good bearing, as well as the admiration and affection of his equals, to whom he was courteous and forbearing. When the regiment was returning to England, the officers frequently spent their leisure time, on board of the man-of-war that brought it home, playing dice. One day, when they were at their games, the Big Lad was look-ing on, and he saw a young man, one of the English officers, insolently, but more in jest than in earnest, striking on the ear the colonel of the regiment, who, the Big Lad knew, was a Highlander. When he saw the insult was not resented, he said in Gaelic to the Colonel, "Why did you let him strike you?" *(C' ar son a leig thu leis do bhualadh?).* "You are, then, a Highlander," the colonel said to him, " and you have been with me for seven years without telling me that you are." " If you would do what I ask you, I will make yon one that he will not do the same thing to you again," he said to the colonel.

"What do you want me to do?" the colonel said. " That you will write out my discharge when we reach London," he said. " But a soldier cannot get his discharge without an order (stamped) under the crown," the colonel said. "Write what you can for me and I will not plead for more," he said. " Anything I can write will not do you any good," the colonel said. " Write that itself," he said ; and he got it written. Next time the play was going on, the Big Lad looked on, and when

he saw the same one striking the colonel again, he went to him
and asked why he did it. The reply he got was that soldiers
were not allowed to question their officers. " This is my way
of excusing myself," the Big Lad said, giving him a blow he
had cause to remember all his life, if he ever recovered from
it. The soldier was sentenced to be severely punished, but on
arriving in England, he deserted—though desertion of the army
is not a custom of Highland soldiers—and became a fugitive.
The great esteem in which he was held prevented any one from
hindering his flight. He got ashore at night among the baggage,
and harbour lights not being numerous in those days, he could
not easily be seen making his escape. Whenever he got his
foot on land he set off, and during the remainder of the night
he ran on flying from pursuit. In the day-time he hid himself
under hedges and haystacks, and next night fled on. On the
following day he was becoming exhausted, and he ventured to
ask food at a wayside house. As his appearance was that of a
poor soldier he got scanty fare, but he asked with civility for
better food, and it was given to him. While he was taking it
two strangers came in to the same room with him, and seeing
his table well supplied while their own was poorly furnished,
one of them said, "It is strange to see a Highland soldier with
good food, while we have next to nothing," and he went over
and swept away all the meat from the soldier's table to his own.
The soldier called the mistress of the house and asked her who
the men were. She said they were travellers, and she asked
them why they took the meat from the soldier's table, and told
them if they had in a civil manner asked better food for themselves they would have got it, instead of raising a quarrel. The
soldier said he would settle the quarrel ; and finding a large
iron hoop *(lùbach mhòr iaruinn)* at hand, he straightened it (a
fathom in length) and flung it round the head of the one
nearest to him, then twisted it in a noose and put the other
one's head in the remainder. He then drew them both out

after him, and left them on the high road. " Now," he said to
them at parting, " you can travel on, for you will not come out
of that tie till you are put in a smithy fire *(teallach gobhainn)."*
He returned to pay the hostess, who said to him, " You do not
appear to have much money." "I have seven day's pay of a
soldier left, to pay my way," he said. " Good youth," she said,
" here is double the amount to you, to take you on your
journey, and I am sufficiently repaid by your ridding my house
of disagreeable guests." He took the gift thankfully, and
turned his face northwards, to come to Scotland *(Albainn).*
The next evening, he saw a fine house, to which he went in the
dusk, and asked permission to warm himself. He was allowed
to enter, aud while standing with his back to the fire, the
daughter of the house saw the handsome stranger, and she told
her father. He desired food to be given to him, and that he was
to be sent where he was. When she went with this request,
the soldier asked who her father was. She said he was a
nobleman *(àrd-dhuin' uasal).* " A soldier is a bad companion
for a nobleman," he said. He went with her and saw her
father, a grey-haired man in a chair, looking about him. The
soldier was asked to sit down. After conversing some time,
the old man said, " Young man, I have a daughter here who
gives me much trouble to keep her in company. If you can
play cards *(iomairt chairtean),* take my place at the table ; there
is a money reward *(duais airgid)* for every game won." "I have no
money," the soldier replied. "I will lend you some," she said. The
play went on till he won six games, one after another. He then
wanted to stop playing, and offered her back all the winnings,
but she would only take the sum she lent him, saying the rest
was rightly his own. He was to remain there that night, and
was not to go away in the morning without telling them. Being
afraid of pursuit, he went away at daybreak. He had not gone
far when he knew that a horseman was coming after him. He
waited to see if he was sent to get back the money he had won

at the card table ; but it was a messenger with a request to him from the nobleman to return to the castle. When he appeared the nobleman chid him for leaving the castle unknown to him, and told him how his daughter had fallen in love with him, and had resolved never to marry any one else. The soldier said, "A soldier is a poor husband for her." The nobleman was convinced that he was not a common soldier whatever circumstances had placed him in that position, and said he preferred his daughter's happiness to wealth or rank. He remained with them and married the daughter ; and when he laid aside the soldier's dress, there was not his equal to be seen in the new dress provided for him. He was esteemed for the dignity of his demeanour as much as he was admired for his fine appearance, and he lived, without remembrance of his past misadventures, in the enjoyment of happiness and prosperity. In those days news travelled slowly, newspapers appearing only once or twice a year in populous villages, and they did not reach remote places. In one which came to the nobleman at this time, there was an account of two men tied in an iron rod *(ann an slait iaruinn)* who were being exhibited at a market town in England. He went with the nobleman and his friends to see this wonder, the two who were in the union *(an dithis a bha 's a' chaigionn)*. Whenever the men saw the Highlander they said to him "If you were dressed in the kilt, we would say you were the man who put us in this noose." "If you had been more civil," he said to them, opening the coil, "when you met me, you would not to-day be fools going through England with an iron rod round your necks." On this he was cheered by the people, and if he was held in esteem before, he was much more on his return home, where he remained and became a great man *(duine mòr)*, beloved and esteemed to the end of his life.

DONALD GORM was at one time in the Island of Skye with his
galley and crew. When returning home to Uist, the day they
set out happened to become very stormy, and stress of weather
obliged them to return and make straight for Dunvegan, the
nearest place of shelter they could reach, where Donald Gorm
was not very willing to go if he could in any way avoid landing
there, since he had killed MacLeod of Dunvegan in a quarrel
which had arisen between them ; but there was no alternative.
On observing the boat coming and in danger of being lost
MacLeod and the men of Dunvegan went to the shore to meet
them, and when they were safely landed gave them a kindly reception. MacLeod took them with him to his castle and provided
hospitably for them. Donald Gorm was invited to MacLeod's
own table, but refused, saying, "When I am away from home,
like this, with my men, I do not separate from them but sit
with them." MacLeod said, "Your men will get plenty of
meat and drink by themselves, and come you with me." "I
will not take food but with my men," he said. When Mac-
Leod saw that Donald Gorm was resolved not to be separated
from his own men, and being unwilling to let him sit with
his, he asked in preference Donald Gorm's men to his own
company. When dinner was over, drinking commenced, and
MacLeod becoming warm said to Donald Gorm by way of
remembrance, "Was it not you who killed my father?" "It
has been laid to my charge that I killed three contemptible
Highland lairds *(tri sgrogainich de thighearnan Gaidhealach)*,
and I do not care though I should put the allegation on its
fourth foot to-night;" Donald Gorm said, drawing his dirk :
"There is the dirk that killed your father; it has a point, a

haft *(faillein)*, and is sharp edged, and is held in the second
best hand at thrusting it in the west."² MacLeod thought he
was the second best hand himself, and he said, "Who is the
other?" Donald Gorm shifted the dagger to his left hand,
raised it, and said, "There it is." MacLeod became afraid
and did not revive any other remembrance. When Donald
Gorm was offered a separate room at night, he said, "Whenever
I am from home I never have a separate bed from my men but
sleep in their very midst until I return to my own house again."
They told him that his men had a sleeping-place provided for
them, and that he would be much better accommodated by
himself in the room prepared for him. When they saw he
could not be persuaded to alter his determination of passing
the night with his men, they made beds for himself and men
in the kiln *(àth)*.³ The men, being wearied, slept without care,
but Donald Gorm did not close an eye. He had a friend,
somehow, in his time of need *(caraid èiginn air chor-eiginn)*, in
the place, who came secretly to the kiln where he and his men
lay, and called to him, "Is it a time to sleep, Donald?" *(An
cadal dhuit, a Dhòmhnuill?)* "What if it is?" *('Dé na 'm b' è?)*,
he answered from within the kiln. "If it is, it will not be"
(na 'm b' è cha bhì), said the one outside. "Waken, men, and
rise quickly," he said to his company. They got up at once
and with all speed went out, shutting the door of the kiln
behind them when they were all through to the outside. They
fled straight to the shore and launched their boat; and fortunate-
ly for them the wind had calmed and they were able to put out
oars and row the galley some distance from the shore before
their flight was observed. They had not gone far to sea before
they saw the kiln on fire. "In place of your father and grandfather you have left yourself without a house, and Donald
Gorm is where you cannot reach him," Donald Gorm said, and
he got safely home to his own house without hurt or injury
(gun bheud gun mhilleadh).

NOTES.

1 The quarrel in which MacLeod was killed was caused, it is said, by Donald Gorm's having repudiated his wife, who was a daughter of MacLeod, in order to marry MacKenzie of Kintail's sister, and MacLeod resenting the insult attacked Donald Gorm, who killed him and his two sons by throwing them over precipices in the Coolin hills in Skye where the skirmish took place. A different version of this incident is given in an early account of the "Troubles in the isles betwixt the Clan Donald and the Seil Tormot, the year 1601," and is to the effect that the feud was carried on by "Sir Rory MacLeod of the Herries," brother-in-law of Donald Gorm MacDonald of Sleat, the reprisals being fierce and frequent until the MacLeods were beaten at "Binguillin," where a brother of Sir Rory and other chief men of his party were taken prisoners by Donald Gorm, but on a reconciliation taking place they were set at liberty. (See Gregory's History of the Western Highlands and Isles, p. 295).

2 In regard to the story and incident of the dagger, there was a song made, of which the writer has only been able to get the following verse :—

> This is the dirk that killed your father,
> And it has not refused you yet,
> Farewell to you from the side of the channel.

> "Holoagaich h-ol-ò
> Sud a' bhiodag a mharbh d' athair,
> 'S cha do dhiùlt i ri thusa fhathast ;
> Soraidh leat o thaobh a' chaoil."

3 Kiln *(àth)* here mentioned was in a thatched house about 17 feet long and 10 wide, the breast being about 5 feet deep, one being built in every township for preparing corn for grinding, Some peacefully disposed, observant old men *(bodaichean sicire foirfe)* built kilns in their own barns, to avoid being hindered or disturbed by their neighbours at their work.

DONALD GORM IN MOIDART.

THE wife of the laird of Moidart *(Bean Mhac 'ic Ailein Mhùideart)* once took great umbrage at Donald Gorm. He came to Mac 'ic Ailein's house, dressed, as was his custom, in a suit of cloth of dun (natural) coloured sheep's wool, with a stout oaken cudgel in his hand. The laird's wife happened to be the first person he met, and without any preliminary word he asked, "Is the lad Mac 'ic Ailein at home?" *(Bheil am balach Mac 'ic Ailein a stigh?)* "No, he is not, at this time," she answered indignantly resenting his superciliousness. The next question he asked was, "Will it be a long time before he comes home?" "I don't know," she said. "You will tell him when he returns home, that I was asking for him here, and that The Herd is the name I get *(gur e am Buachaille a their iad rium)."* Mac 'ic Ailein came home soon afterwards, and his wife told him about the bold man who was enquiring. At her husband's request she described the stranger's appearance and dress, and how "The Herd" was the name he got. "Did you ask him in?" her husband asked. "No," she said, "he was so impertinent." "None but me will pay the penalty for that," he said, "for he was Donald Gorm of Sleat" *(Dòmhnull Gorm Shlèibhte).* Mac 'ic Ailein desired a horse to be saddled, and he rode at full speed after, and overtook, Donald Gorm at the inn. After much entreaty he was persuaded to return to Mac 'ic Ailein's house. On their arrival his wife made ample apology, and the friendship was not broken.

Mac 'ic Ailein had to hold MacConnel, the Herd of the Isles *(Mac Chonnuill Buachaille nan Eileinean)* stirrup at every feast and fair.

THE BLACK RAVEN OF GLENGARRY.

THE boundary line between the estates of Glengarry and Kintail was, for ages, a winding river (*amhuinn cham*, literally "crooked river") which often overflowed its banks, changed its course, and made encroachments on the land, sometimes on one side and as frequently on the other, causing disputes and quarrels, in regard to their respective rights and limits, between the proprietors of the estates which it separated; the tenantry (*an tuath*) on each property taking the part of their chief when the strife ran high. In order to put an end to the quarrelling the Chief of Glengarry (*Mac 'Ic Alasdair*) at this time insisted on a straight line being drawn to mark the boundary between them, but MacKenzie of Kintail would not give his assent to any proposal for changing the old line which followed the course of the river, and the feud broke out afresh (*bha an tabaid air a bonn a rithist*). Glengarry had three sons, and in the skirmish that took place on that occasion the two eldest sons were killed. The youngest having been left at home on account of his youth, escaped the fate of his brothers. He became known afterwards as the Black Raven of Glengarry. When he grew up to manhood his father said to him one day, "An insulting message (*fios tàmailteach*) has been sent to me from Kintail about the boundary line, and I must accept the challenge and gather the men, and you must go with us." "If it is fighting you have in view," said the Raven, "you must do it yourself, for me; my two dear brothers were killed through your foolish quarrels, and I would have been killed also if I had been old enough to be with them at the time, but since I can now understand how trifling the cause is, I will let yourselves be fighting." His father could only gather his men and go to the contest without

him.   When they were out of sight, the Raven put on his best
suit of armour and took several turns round the hill to elude
the notice of any straggler who might have been left, and then
set off at his utmost speed to get in advance of his father and
men.   Before evening closed he was at the head of Loch
Duich, where he passed the night.   Next day he procured a
plaid of MacKenzie tartan which he wrapped round him to
disguise the red badge *(suaicheantas dearg)* of Glengarry, and
made his way to the enemy's headquarter's at Donan Isle
(Eilean donnan), where the Kintail men were rapidly gathering
to the fray.   It was customary in those days to set a large long
table *(bòrd mòr fada)* supplied with abundance of food and
drink for the entertainment of the men who assembled from
far and near.   The Chief sat at the head, and every man on
taking his place stuck his dirk *(biodag)* in the edge of the table
in front of him before sitting down.   The Black Raven got in
among the men unnoticed, and when the Chief of Kintail came
in, he said to the man who was beside him, " I wish to sit next
to Kintail."   His appearance did not betray him, and no one
objected to his request, but when he was taking the seat beside
the Chief, he threw MacKenzie backwards on the ground and
put his foot upon him to keep him down, and the point of his
dirk resting on the breast of the prostrate man.   His plaid having
slipped aside, the red *(an dearg)* was exposed, and in an instant
a hundred dirks were ready to riddle him *(g' a dheanamh 'n a
chriathar-tholl);* but he said, commanding them, "The moment
I am approached, your Chief will be a dead man."   " If I fall,"
he said to the Chief, "it will be on the hilt of my own weapon,
and you will never rise—its point is on your breast, and any
attempt to take my life imperils yours.   I did not come here
for war but for peace, and unless you will consent to lay aside
all animosities, and solemnly promise never to renew this
quarrel, your life is forfeited.   I have only to press the hilt of
this dagger, on which my hand rests, and whatever fate awaits

me you will have no more power to do harm." Kintail agreed to make peace, and gave his oath twice on the cold iron of the dirk on his breast that he would faithfully keep his promise. The Black Raven, after sharing in the hospitalities provided for the occasion, returned home, the Chief and men of Kintail accompanying him part of the way. When he met his father with his band of fighting men, he told them to return home, that he had done alone more than they had ever been able to do with all their boasting and fighting ; he had put an end to their fighting, and got a guarantee for a lasting peace without one drop of bloodshed, and henceforth if he found any one among them making or renewing the quarrel, he would give the Chief of Kintail full liberty to treat them as he saw proper.

The friendship then made between the Chieftains was ever afterwards steadily maintained by them, and the Raven became one of the most distinguished men in the service of his country at that time.

CAILLEACH POINT, OR THE OLD WIFE'S HEADLAND,

Is one of the stormiest and most dangerous headlands on the west coast of Scotland. From base to top it is rocky, and for a considerable distance on each side.

It faces the Island of Coll, and commands a view of the Point of Ardnamurchan, from which it is distant about seven or eight miles. At its base there is a strong tidal channel which has never been known to be dry at the lowest ebb tide. From its highest point the spectre of "Hugh of the Little

E

Head " is said to cross on horseback to Coll to give warning, as he is wont to do, to any descendants of the house of Loch-buie of their approaching end.   Hugh is said to have had his head cut off by a broad sword in one of the clan skirmishes of old times.   He has his head in a blaze of fire, and the tracks of his horse seen on the snow shew only three legs, and the terror of children and credulous people is increased by his being said to drag a chain after him.   To the south of the Point there is a cave, which becomes accessible only when the tide has half fallen.   Its Gaelic name is *Uamh Bhuaile nan Drogh.*   Wild pigeons tenant it, and are seen emerging when the tide has fallen.   The cooing sound of the birds heard under water seems to have led to the name, which means, the Cave of the Cattle-fold of the fairies, and it is noticeable that the word *Drogh* denotes that it first received its name from a Teutonic source, very possibly from the race that came ulti-mately to tenant the Orkney islands.   It is said, however, that Dutchmen possessed the fisheries on the west coast of Scotland, and it has been suggested that the word *Drogh* is from Drag-net, which they kept in the cave.   The tides which sweep past this point render it more difficult and dangerous to get past in a head wind than even the Point of Ardnamurchan, of which the dangerous character is well known.   To the north of the Point in the direction of Croig in Mull, there is an indentation which is called *Achlais na Caillich* (the old woman's oxter or armpit) where salmon nets are set.   It has been characterised as not the armpit of a smooth woman *(Achlais na mnà mìne)* and the story which is said to have given its name to the Headland, is, that an old woman was gathering shell-fish in the neighbourhood when the tide began to make, and the woman finding no other means of escape made a last effort by climbing up the rocks.   When at the top, and almost out of danger, she said " I am safe now, in spite of God and men " *(Tha mi tearuinte nis ge b' oil le Dia 's le daoine).*   She was converted into a stone forming part of the rock distinctly to be seen from the highest point of *Cailleach*. It is said that the figure of the old woman was very distinctly to be seen at first, and hence the name of the Headland, but time has done its own work and the figure is not now so unmistakable. Even the origin of the name is only known to those who are natives of the neighbourhood.

On one occasion, the writer being himself ensconced under the side deck of a smack, then plying to the island, heard a Tiree boatman, who was conversing with a minister from the south of Argyleshire, and had no fancy for the overly pious talk of the too-zealous stranger, remarking that there was an old woman here and when she gave a snort, she could be heard over in Coll. ["*Tha Cailleach an so 's trà nì i sreothart cluinnidh iad 'an Cola i.*"] The minister said that that was most extra-ordinary, and as it now began to rain the boatman began to exhort him to go below, and professed much regard for the minister's health. At last he got rid of him.

A TRADITION OF ISLAY.

THE western isles according to tradition were thinly inhabited for a long period of years, after the defeat and expulsion of the Norsemen. These invaders had left few of the natives alive and the land remained desolate. The first man then who took possession of the country was powerful John MacConnal who was called, the shepherd of the isles, and the first of the lords of the isles (*Iain mòr Maconuil ris an abairteadh buachaille nan eileanan, b'e ceud tighearna nan eileanan).* He had seven sons, among whom, when they came of age, he began to divide his possessions, but the Highlands and isles being too limited in his opinion for division among so many, he went away to Ireland with one of his sons, to overthrow one or more of the five kings by whom that country was then governed, and put his son in possession of any territory he might acquire in the contest, leaving his eldest son in Islay, which was the first of the isles possessed by him. In this enterprise he succeeded in seizing that part of Ireland then under the authority of the Earl of Antrim, and gave it to his son, whose nephew came from Islay, when some years had passed, to see him in Antrim. This nephew during one of those visits fell in love with a noblewoman of the country whom he asked in marriage. His proposal being agreed to, he was requested, as was then the custom, to name the dowry he wanted with her. His request was 700 men who had nicknames *(far-ainmeannan)* to take with him to Islay. In those days, it is said, that great men and nobles only had pseudonyms and he took this method of getting these and their followers to repeople the isles, and their descendants are yet to be found in many parts of the country as well as in the islands.

NOTES.

Islay is separated from the island of Jura by the sound of Islay and lies west of Cantyre in Argyleshire. Its extent is 25 miles long and 17 miles broad. The south west point is called the Rhinns *(an roinn Ileach)*. The island is hilly and penetrated by an arm of the sea, Lochindaal, which is 12 miles long and 8 miles broad. There are good crops grown on the island and cattle are reared and fish is abundant on its coasts. A small quantity of various kinds of ore is found throughout the island, but its distilleries are its chief industry at the present day. It was in former times the chief residence of the Lords of the Isles, and the ruins of castles, forts, and chapels are numerous and interesting as records of a past age.

The Beatons or Bethunes and MacLarty are said to have been among those who came from Ireland with *MacConuil*. The latter being descendants of grey haired Niel (*Nial Liath*) who was interpreter (*fear-labhairt*) for Maconnal, hence the name. It is told of Niel, that being at one time surrounded by his enemies in a battle, he was commanded to deliver his sword. "If I do, he said, it will be by the point" (*ma liubhras, 'sann an aghaidh a ranna*), and cleaving his way through them he escaped and joined his companions.

After his settlement in the western island MacConnal (*Iain Mòr MacConuill*) is said to have divided his possessions among his seven sons by sending one of them John (*Iain*) to Glencoe, hence the patronymic Clan of the son of John of Glencoe (*Clann 'ic Iain Ghleann-a-comhunn*), another son Ronald (*Raonull*) was sent to Keppoch (*a' Cheapaich*), one Allan (*Ailean*) was sent to Moidart (*Mùideart*). These were settled on the mainland in the counties of Argyle and Inverness, while the island of Skye was given to another son, Grim Donald of Sleat, (*Dòmhnull gorm Shléibhte*). Another son got the smaller isles, and another went to Ireland and became Earl of Antrim while the heir remained in Islay and held the adjacent islands as well as portions of the mainland. Of the 700 who returned with his son from Antrim to people the islands after the expulsion of the Norsemen, 22 were heads of families. The person from whom the writer heard this, now above 70 years of age, was certain that Beaton or Bethune was one of the names, but he had forgotten the others.

FAIR LACHLAN, SON OF FAIR NEIL OF DERVAIG.

(Lachunn fionn mac Neill bhàin, Fear Dhearbhaig.

At the time when Lachlan Kattanach was Chief of MacLean *(ri linn Mhic-'illeathain Lachunn Cattanach na gruaige)*, his wife *(a bhantighearna)* dreamt about an Irish chief of the name of William O'Power (?) *(Uilleam O' buaidh)* and in the same way, at the same time, this Irish Chief dreamt about her. It happened then that they began to communicate with each other. (At that time more trade was carried on with Ireland by these Western Isles than with any other place.) One day MacLean discovered that his wife was keeping on a correspondence, unknown to him, with the Irish Chief, and was much distressed about this injury to his honour. In order to test his wife's affection for her secret lover, he went to her with a penknife in his hand and said, " There is a present *O' buaidh* has sent you " She looked at the knife and said,

> " My darling who sent me the knife
> I weary at his delay in coming across the sea,
> And may I not enjoy health
> If I do love it better than the hand that holds it."

> (M' eudail 'chuir thugam an sgian
> 'S fhada leam a thriall thar muir,
> 'S na 'n a mheall mi mo shlàint'
> Mur docha leam i na 'n lamh 'sa bheil).

MacLean was then convinced of his wife's disgrace, and went away and sent for his kinsman, Fair Lachlan *(Lachunn fionn)* who was then at Hynish, and who, on receiving a message from his Chief, went immediately to Island House. On reaching, MacLean said to him, " I sent for you to go to Ireland; you are a clever man and you have seven sons, go and bring me the head of O'Power, and any crime you may commit, or any

injustice you may from this time do to any one, will be over
looked by me *(tha thu 'n ad dhuine tapaidh 's seachdnar mhac
agad, falbh 's thoir g' am ionnsuidh ceann Uilleam O' buaidhe 's
aona chron na anaceart sam bith nì thu theid a mhathadh dhuit
leamsa).* Next day, *Lachunn fionn* with his sons set off in the
galley, and before sundown he was in Islay. The following day he
was in Ireland, and asked the first person he met for the man he
was tracing *(a bha e air a luirg).* "If you wish to see him," the
person said, "he is coming this way, in a coach drawn by two
white horses, and no one in Ireland has that but himself." The
old man then went on to try and meet him, and after going a short
distance he saw him coming towards him to meet him *(chaidh
an sean duine air aghaidh feuch an tachradh e air, 's an ceann
ceum na dhà chunnaic e e tighinn 'na choinneamh 's 'na chòmhail).*
When he came near, O'Power *(O' buaidh)* commanded him to
stop, and said, "I see you are a stranger in the place?"
"Indeed," he replied, *(seadh ars' esan).* "Whence have you
come?" the Chief asked, *(Co ás a thàinig thu?).* "I came
from Tiree," he answered. "Do you know the lady of Mac-
Lean there?" "I know her well," he said. "Will you bring
her a message from me?" *(An toir thu fios uam g' a h-ionns-
uidh?)* "I will," he said, *(bheir, ars' esan).* The chief there
and then put the message in order, and put his head out of
the coach to deliver it, but the other, while taking it with the
one hand, struck off his head with the other hand. *(Sin fhéin
chuir e 'n teachdaireachd air doigh 's chuir e mach a cheann g' a
toirt dà, 's 'nuair bha e 'ga gabhail leis an aona laimh thilg e dheth
an ceann leis an laimh eile).* The man-servant was stupified
(lit. went astray), *(chaidh an gille air seacharan),* and Fair
Lachlan got an opportunity *(fhuair e fàth)* of taking the head
with him to the galley with which he set sail *(leig e ri cuain di)*
and was in Islay on his return journey that evening. Next day
after *(maireach 'na dheighinn sin)* he was in Tiree, and went
early in the day to Island House *(do 'n cilean).* Finding, on

reaching, that MacLean and his wife were at breakfast, he went
in where they were and put the head of the Irish Chief on the
end of the table, with the face towards MacLean's wife. She
looked at it and fell down stone dead at the side of the table
(sheall i air 's thuit i fuar marbh aig taobh a' bhùird). Some
time after this Fair Lachlan's sons were taking peats home
from Moss to Hynish. There were five of them with seven
horses, which were fastened together, and went on one after
another, having a sort of deep basket *(cliabh)* slung on each side
of each horse for the conveyance of burdens. On account of
Big Dewar of Balemartin, who was so fierce, *(co fiadhaich)* they
could not take the straight way by Balemartin to Hynish, but
had to take the more rugged path by Hynish hill, where, at
Creag nan cliabh (Creel rock) the footpath was so narrow that
on these occasions a person was in waiting to be in readiness
to take the creels off the horses and carry them past the rock.
At that time, there was a mill past Balviceon, with a bridge
across the dam which had to be lifted before sundown, and on
their way they had to pass across the bridge. It happened
on this occasion that the young men, by their own folly *(le 'n
amaideachd fhein)*, were later than usual of returning, and the
bridge was withdrawn; and with the speed with which they
were going on, they did not observe that the bridge was lifted,
and the foremost of the horses went headlong into the dam
and was choked *(air a thachdadh).* The lads made their
way home, and told their father how the miller had taken
away the bridge, and what had happened to them. He
said, "If my horse was choked on his account *(air a thàillibh)*,
the same thing will be done to him to-night yet"; and
that was what happened. He and his sons went back the
same way, step by step, *(air a' cheart cheum)*, and they caught
the poor man while he was asleep *(rug iad air an duine 'na
leabaidh)* and took him with them and hung him on the hillock
of the cross *(bac na croiche)*, opposite Island House. When a

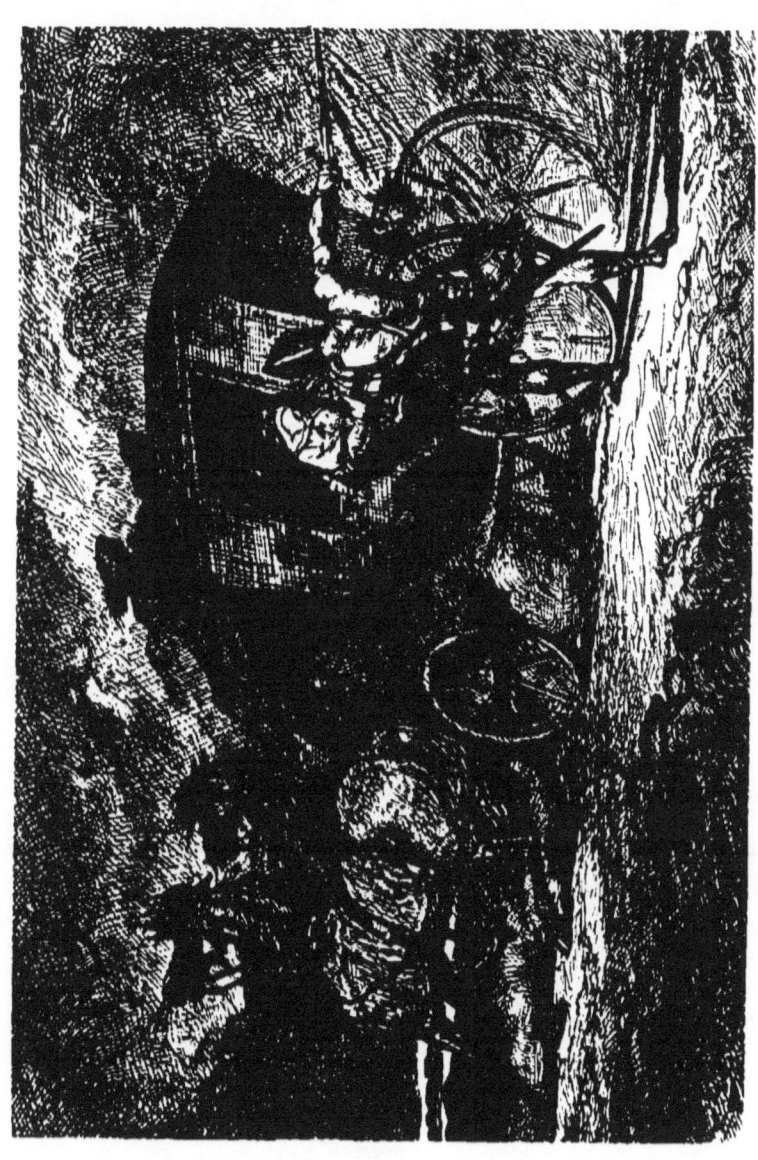

THE MESSAGE DELIVERED TO THE LOVER AND THE MANNER OF HIS DEATH.

servant went in early next morning to kindle a fire in the room where MacLean was, he asked what sort of day it was. The servant said that it was a good day, but that a strange sight was to be seen *(ni a tha cuir ioghnadh mór orm ri fhaicinn).* "What is that?" the Chief asked. "It is a man hung on the hillock up yonder *(duine air a chrochadh air a' chroich shuas ud).* MacLean said, as he rose up, "Who or what person dared do this without my permission? *(Co an aona duine 'san dùthaich aig an robh 'chridh leithid so dheanamh gun chuir 'nam cheadsa?)* When he saw the deed that was done, he shed bitter tears, and said that no one had done this but Fair Lachlan *(cha d' rinn duine riamh so ach Lachunn fionn).* "It was in the agreement I made with him when he brought me the man's head from Ireland." This was the last hanging that was done in the island *(b'e so an crochadh mu dheireadh a rinneadh 's an eilean).*

LEGENDARY HISTORY.

PRINCESS THYRA OF ULSTER AND HER LOVERS.

A STORY OF LOCHMAREE.[1]

AT one time the King of Denmark is said to have sent his son to the Scottish court along with six others *(seisear eile)*. They landed in Caithness, where, as they came chiefly for sport, they began to look for deer and other wild animals, and to enquire where they were to be found. They were told that all animals of the chase had become scarce since more people had come to that part, but that in the neighbouring parts of the country, especially in Ross-shire, they were still numerous, and if they went there they would get abundant sport. They went, and while they remained lived in a house of the MacKenzies', near Lochmaree. One day then, when following deer in the hill, the young prince got separated from his companions, who each and all found their way safely home. When he came in sight of the house, being fatigued, he sat down by the roadside and fell asleep. He was awakened by the sound of voices, and on looking he saw two men, one of whom was young and the other old, coming on the road towards him with a young woman walking between. He got up, and as they were coming nearer he was making out that he never saw a more beautiful woman. He stood before them and spoke. The old man said, "You are doing wrong in delaying us on our way." "Methinks," said the young prince, , "that I am not doing any thing out of the way, nor have I spoken a wrong word." The old man got angry, and calling him rough names said he was ill-bred. "That was not the way in which I was taught," the prince answered,

" I have the blood of the kings of Denmark in my veins, and I am inclined to put your head as low as your shoes for your ill words *(air son do dhroch bheul)* which I have not deserved." When the old man heard this he became afraid, and made excuses for the warmth of temper he had shewn, but said he was under vows to protect the girl from all intrusion, "the reason being that she is with us under the vows of the church *(fo naomhachadh na h-eaglais)*, by her father's commands," and told him that they came ashore from the monastery of Isle-maree and were to return before nightfall. " I would like well to know who the maiden is whom you befriend," said the young prince. "The name of the daughter is," the old man answered, " Princess Thyra *(Deorath)* of the house of Ulster in Ireland—and let us now pass." In the parting the young prince said to the maiden, " As this has been our first meeting, so I fear it is to be our last: Farewell!" " I do not say," she answered. He went home, but, after some days, returned to the same place expecting to see the same company, but no one came ashore from the islet that day. The next time he went he waited two days in vain, and the third time three days, and returned home in the same way ill-pleased at his mischance. He then resolved to go to the isle if there was a way of getting io it. He was told that a man on the other side of the loch had a boat, and he went to him and got him to go with him. On landing, the man pointed out to him the way to the monas-tery, and told him that he would come to a well, which he was not to pass till he drank of its water; that the well was famed for its efficacy in every malady to which mankind is subject, and especially in restoring those who had lost their reason; "and beside the well," said the man, "there is a tree with a hollow in its side *(slochd 'n a taobh)*, and no one goes past it without putting something of more or less value in." The youth went ashore, and, heedless of tree and well, reached the house and demanded admittance at the first door he met.

When asked what brought him, or why he came, he said he came to see the Irish princess. He was told that could not be *(ni nach gabhadh deanamh).* He then asked if there was any one in authority of whom he could make the request, and was told there was the oldest of rank in the monastery, who, when he came, said, "No! you cannot see the princess." The young man then told who he was, and said, "If I want her for my wife and she consents, can you prevent the union?" "We will leave the matter to her own will," the old man answered. She came gladly, and the prince spent that day on the islet. Before he left she said, "I have a doubt in this matter." "What is that?" he asked. "It is that I never saw you but once before now, neither did you see me, and if love comes quickly, it may go as quickly." "You know that from yourself," he said. "No," she answered. He told her to look at the evening star, which was to be seen in the south-western sky, and said, "As truly as that star shines on yonder hill, so truly do I love you." "I have another doubt," she said. "Your doubts are very many," he said. Her doubt was, that Red Hector of the hills, as he was called from being among the hills day and night, would be a dangerous foeman if he met him on his way. He returned, landed, and having cause, as he thought, to be pleased with events, was going on joyously and light-hearted, whistling as he went along. He was not far on his way when an arrow passed close to his face; the next one stuck in his bonnet. He stood looking about him and saw a big man standing beside a rock that was at the roadside before him. "What sort of man are you, when you are going to make a target of me?" the prince said. "Have you never heard of Red Hector of the hills *(Eachann Ruadh nan cnoc)?* If you have not, you now see him and will feel his skill. There is a matter to settle between us which can never be done but in one way, and that is, that you kill me or I kill you." They took their swords, one each *(claidheamh an t-aon),* blood was

shed; the prince then asked if there was no other way of
settling the matter except by bloodshed. " Do not waste
speech *(Na bi 'cosg do sheanachais)*; that you kill me or I kill
you, there is no other way," he said, and struck the prince on
the side with his sword and sorely wounded him. He fell and
his enemy fled. The wounded man kept his hand on the
wound, but whenever he moved the blood spurted from it, and
he was passing the night in that way till his tongue became
swollen in his mouth. In the midst of his agony he heard the
drip of a streamlet in the hollow underneath where he lay, and
tried to move himself towards it, but could not, though he
made every effort. At last he thought it was better to bleed to
death than die of thirst, and by dragging himself along he
reached the water, but before he got to drink of it he fainted
and lay beside the streamlet till next day, when those, the
humane people *(na daoine cneasda)*, who came ashore in the
boat heard his moaning, and recognising him, took him back
to the islet, where he remained unconscious for many weeks,
during which his own men, who had been brought to the isle,
and the princess attended him. When he recovered and knew
that the maiden's constant care and watchfulness had helped to
restore him to life, he expressed much gratitude. "When you
are up and well," she said, "it will be time to thank me." He
kept telling her every day how he would take her to Denmark.
One day then a ship was seen coming, from which a boat was
sent ashore to take away the maiden, whose father lay dying.
"Will you return?" he said. "I will return," she said. "And
you will not forget me among your own people." "Nothing
but death will prevent my return," she said. She went away,
and nothing was heard of her for many days. In his impatience
the prince sent men from day to day to the top of the highest
hills to look for the ship. At last they saw three ships coming,
and the first had the royal flag of Ireland in its topmast. Some
time before the maiden left the islet, the prince one day when

on land met an old man who intercepted him ; his men bade
the intruder keep to one side of the road, but the man refused
to be put aside, and the prince then asked what his business
was with him. " Do not speak so gruffly," the old man said,
" I have come to you, as I am in need of shelter, to ask if you
will take me into your service while you are here." " My
burden is on others at present," the prince said, "and little an
old man like you with a staff in his hand can do to help me.
Have you a house or home ?" " I had till yesterday; to-day I
have nothing. I had house, wife, son, land, cattle, and yesterday every beast that I had was lifted, except a stray sheep, and
my son went in search of it and fell over the rocks *(chaidh am
balach leis na creagan)* and was killed. When his mother heard
what had happened to him she went to the place, and on seeing
her son dead she leapt in the sea and was drowned, and I am
left alone. If you will take me with you I will do you more
service in the hills than a younger man can do." He said his
name was MacKenzie *(Dùghall MacChoinnich)*. The prince
took him to be with them while they remained in the isle.

When the ships were seen the prince went to the highest
summit of the hills, taking with him, among the rest, the old
man, who on their way said, " Delay *(air do shocair)*, till I tell
you my dream." " I care naught for dreams," the other said.
" Will you not listen, for I dreamt the same dream three nights
after each other; and it was that she was dead." "We wish to
get joyous news and you have given us instead news of sorrow."
The old man then said, " I will go to the ship, and when I
reach, if all is well you will see a red signal, and if sorrow
awaits you it will be a black one." He went, and on reaching,
she was there. She knew him and asked if all was well. He
told her, and she said, " He is impatient for news." He then
persuaded the princess, against her own will and the advice of
those around her, to shew the death-signal, saying the joy of
seeing her living would compensate her lover for the deception.

When the signal was seen by those on land, the prince said he could no longer live, and took his dagger from its sheath and killed himself. When the princess reached the shore, those who met her told her how her lover, believing that she was dead, had killed himself. She asked where he was, and said that no seen or unseen power could prevent her from taking a last farewell, and that she would go alone and do no injury to herself. When she was going in where the dead body lay, she noticed that some one was following her, and turning she saw that the intruder was the old man, "Wretched Dugall *(a dhroch Dhùghaill)*, what evil advice you gave me." "That is not my name," he said, "I am Red Hector of the hills, and this is my revenge!" and he killed her with his dirk. He then disappeared and was never seen or heard of in the country after that time.

Note.

1. Lochmaree is in the west of Ross-shire. It lies S.E. and N.W., and has 24 islets throughout its length of about 18 miles. Its breadth is from one to two miles, and its depth prevents its water from freezing.

GARLATHA.

A TRADITION OF HARRIS.

At one time it is said the outermost of the western isles formed three separate and independent possessions; the northern part of the Long Island *(an t-eilean fada)*, Lewis *(Leòdhais)*, was held by one Cenmal *(Ceannamhaol* [baldhead]*)*, who was a king, while the southern portion, Harris *(na h-Earra)*, was owned by a prince; and another king, one named Keligan [thin one], possessed Uist, which is further south. In this way Lewis and Uist had each a king, while there was only a prince in Harris. This prince, who was famed for his courage and bravery, was held in great esteem by those on his land for the good advice *(na comhairlean dealbhach)* they readily got from him and the benefits he conferred on them. He discouraged bickerings and jealousy *(farmad)* among his subordinates and neighbours, and spread among them a knowledge of many useful arts. He encouraged manual labour as well as manly exercise and the recitation of poems, romance, etc. His wife, Garlatha, was not less namely for her goodness to those around her, among whom she promoted thrifty and industrious habits, and taught the use and methods of preparing different kinds of roots, grain and plants, for food and healing, and to be kind and tender to the weak and infirm, and to live good lives. In this way the people on their land were contented with their condition and sought no change. Garlatha died, it is said, about 800 A.D.—a long time ago, but whatever it was, she went away, (and it was not to be helped), leaving an infant daughter who was named after her mother, Garlatha. As the girl grew up it was seen that she inherited her mother's good gifts, and the people were equally well pleased with her. In time she began to be spoken about and heard of, and was sought in marriage by numerous suitors. The king who ruled in Lewis was eager in pursuit of her *('an tòir oirre),* and crossed over to see her. The ruler *(fear-riaghlaidh)* of Uist came on the same errand. One day then her father said to her, "Daughter, I wish to see you married, before the end of my life comes, to a good man, and I am looking to see which of those men who come to see you is the most suitable. and I see that it will suit you best to take him who is in Lewis." His daughter preferred the one who owned Uist, but by her father's advice word was sent to the possessor of Lewis to come and that he would get her. He came, and being well pleased with his reception every arrangement was made, and they were married. Afterwards the bride said to a maid, "You will go in to the entertainment *(fleadh)* and among the company : I am going to hide myself." This was done, and the company sat at the feast without the bride, for whose coming a long delay was made. When it was seen that she would not return, the question of what had become of her or where she was, was asked of every one, but no one knew. The maid was asked, but she had not any knowledge or tale *(fios no sgeul)* to tell of where the lost one was to be found. The time was passing *(bha 'n ùineachd 'ruith)* and search was made outside for her, but she was not fouud. Then they looked for her from place to place, where it was possible to find her, but without success. The night passed, leaving the feast untouched and the guests cheerless. Next day the search was renewed along the shores and among the hills, and in every direction from day to day, till there was not a spot between Barra Head and the Butt of Lewis where a bird could sleep, that was not searched, but there was no trace of her *(cha d' fhuaireadh riamh i, cha d' fhuaireadh idir i).* The father continued to wander about, searching in vain, for many years after all hope of finding her

F

was dead, till at last he was seen to turn every leaf he met with the staff in his hand, and even to look under ragweed *(buagh-allan)*. He died, and she was not found. The place, Harris, was then 200 years without any one to own it *(thug an t-àite sin dà cheud bliadhna gun duine ann)*. MacLeod *(fear Mac Leòid)* then took possession of the country and began to build new houses ; the old dwellings had become uninhabitable *(air dol fàs)* ; the roof had fallen in *(thuit an ceann 'n am broinn)*. When clearing out one of these an old chest was found, and on lifting it the lower part remained on the ground, with the skeleton of a woman resting in it, each bone according to its place *(cnàimh a rèir cnàimh)*, and by its side the wedding-ring, as new as it was on the day it was put on her finger, with the name "Garlatha" engraved on it, and from that the story came.

NOTE.

1. The Long Island includes the whole of the land between the Butt of Lewis and Barra Head.

STORIES ABOUT THE FAIRIES.

THE TRADITION OF A HOUSEWIFE AND HER FAIRY VISITOR.

THE incidents of this tradition are said to have happened in Lewis, but the readiness with which similar stories are appropriated and localised makes it improbable that the circumstances occurred in any special locality. In this instance the person from whom the story was heard being a native of Lewis will account for the incidents of the story having been said to have taken place in that Island. The story is as follows:—

The wife of a tenant farmer, who lived with his family in an extremely remote and hilly rough district, was frequently left alone in the house, as she had no daughters, while her husband and sons were away at the labour of the farm, or fishing. It happened one day after they had left, that the housewife having finished her housework, sat as usual at the spinning-wheel to spin thread for cloth *(clò)* for their clothing. She had not long begun her labour, when, happening to look towards the door, she saw a little woman of reddish appearance coming in at the door with a dog before and one after her. "Woman," she said, "you are spinning." "I am," the housewife answered. "Will you give me a drink of water?" she said. "Take it yourself," the housewife said. "The water is good, where is the well?" she asked. "It is down," said the one who was in, "in the opening of the hollow of the glen *(aig dorus 'an lag a' ghlinne)."* The fay woman *(a' bhean-shìth)* then asked the housewife to lend her a small cauldron, and the other woman believing her to be sister-in-law or some other relative she did not know of the wife of her nearest neighbour, who lived far distant from them and was married to an Ardnamurchan woman, said to her, "There is a table there with several utensils *(caigionn choireachan)* on its shelf; take with you any of them that will answer." When she brought it, she asked for the suspender *(bùlas)* and lid. The moment she got them she fitted them in and told the dogs that were with her to take that with them. The dogs immediately caught the three-legged pot and took it with them. When her husband came home the housewife said, "I think there is a stranger with our neighbours," and told him about her visitor. "Perhaps," her husband said, "she is the sister-in-law; it was time some one came to see the wife, for none of her friends have been since she came here." "I never saw the sort of dogs she had, ever here," his wife said, and described to him the dogs and how they were different altogether from sheep-dogs. "Our neighbours have only one dog and it is a sheep-dog," he said. This day passed and another and the third, but the cauldron was not returned. The housewife then sent one of her sons to ask the neighbours to return the loan. These said that they did not get a loan of anything, as they did not require it, having more cauldrons and kettles than was required by themselves, and that no strangers had come or were with them. The housewife was at her wit's end and did not know in the world or time to come *(uile bheatha na dìlinn)* what to think about the matter. On the fifth day, however, the self-same one returned with the cauldron. "I am sure," she said, "that you were missing the cauldron." "I was," the housewife replied, "not from any need I had of it at the time, but because I did not know who the one was that took it away." "I am sure you did not know who took it," said the one that came in, "but I knew you too well; many a day you sang songs above my house *('s iomadh latha 'sheinn thu luinneag air mullach an tigh agam)."* "Will you sit?" said the one who was spinning. "I will sit and tell my story if you are sure that no one will

come in while I am here." As was customary in those days
the byre adjoined the dwelling-house, whatever kind of wall
(*sgàth-balla*) separated them, and one of the cows that had
calved and was in the byre, made a disturbance *(straighlich)*.
The next look the woman took she was alone. On her
husband's return, she said, "You may not leave me here alone ;
one of the children must be left with me or I will be where
you are ;" and she told him about the second time her strange
visitor came and how suddenly she had disappeared. The
goodman then went for advice to one, the minister, who he
knew was able to give him good counsel. On telling about the
undesirable visitor his wife had, the advice he got was that he
was to pull down his house as quickly as possible, and to put it
at the other end of the land ; "and when you will pull down
your house, every particle *(h-uile pioc)* of the thatch that covers
it is to be burnt within the rafters on which nine cogfuls of sea-
water or charmed (*naoi cuachan sàile no uisge coisrigte*) is to be
poured." The goodman returned home with this advice.
When his wife heard it she said that she must get women to
help her to finish the cloth she was working at, and it was agreed
to give her the help she required. On account of the dampness
of the houses the method of keeping the thread and wool dry
was by hanging them up to the rafters. Next morning the
goodwife missed a pile of wool from its place, but believing
that it was her son, who often played pranks on her, who had
removed it, she said nothing regarding its disappearance. Next
day, however, she was astonished at seeing her late strange
visitor with another and a taller one coming in. "I am sure,"
said the little redhued one, "you were missing the bag of wool
We took it with us to help you, and there it is brought home
made into thread, and your own thread that we took with us for
a pattern (*leth-bhreac*); and any time you have thread to spin,
we are ready to help you." The goodwife was overcome with
fear and could not utter a word to them. They went away, and

she never saw themselves or their shadow (*an dubh no 'n dath*) ever afterwards.   The house was taken down and another was built where they chose it to be, but after some time an old man saw five of the fairy company leaving the well at the foot of the glen, each carrying a vessel full of water, and the place where he saw them going in and lost sight of them, was afterwards quarried, and the stone taken from it was employed to build a church that stands at the present day.   An opening that was met with, in the quarry, where human bones were found, was supposed to be the place where the fairy band entered their dwelling.

THE WISE WOMAN OF DUNTULM AND
THE FAIRIES.

A LORD of the Isles, Mac Connal *(Buachaille nan Eileinean)*, long ago had two sons, but only one could get the estate at his death.   When that happened the eldest son said one day to the youngest, "You are now left without anything, but, that you may not be altogether portionless, go to Duntulm and you will get there a piece of land that you will have to yourself."   The lands of Duntulm, in the northern part of the Island of Skye, were at that time occupied by a prosperous tenantry, consisting chiefly of crofters and the holders of a few larger farms.   The youngest brother was told that the rent he would get from these tenants would maintain him, and he was to build a house and marry a wife. He agreed to go to Duntulm, where he was not a long time settled till a claim was made on his land for the king's dues, the crown tax being in proportion to the amount of land which he held. The first time the tax *(a' chis)* was asked, he said, in answer to the demand which was made, "I will not pay any tax. Why should I pay it? What right has the king to get it?" An order was sent to him every year for payment of the tax, but if it was, for six years he did not pay any of it *(cha do phàidh e sgillinn).* At last the king sent fifty soldiers and one officer to take the rent from him in spite of him *(thar 'amhaich),* and since he would pay to neither king nor soldier, the lands were taken from him and they were now attached to the crown. The king was receiving the revenue, and a Skye carl *(bodach Sgitheanach)* called John Donaldson MacWilliam *(Iain Mac Dhòmhnuill 'ic Uilleim)* was appointed a factor to collect the rents from the crofters. He lived sixteen miles from Duntulm, among the crofts, where he went twice a year to gather the tax. MacConnal's castle was built on a precipitous bank, on the west side of which there was a big pit into which every high tide sent a flow of water that kept it always full, forming a deep pool *(glumag)* that sometimes proved dangerous to the unwary. One day it happened that whatever a crofter, one Macrury, was doing at the castle, he fell headlong into the pool, and however it was, whether he was killed by the fall or drowned, he was found dead next day anyhow. He left two sons who were not of age to help their widowed mother, for whom much sympathy was felt by her neighbours on account of her being left so helpless *(bha i air a fàgail cho lom).* Next spring after this the two lads were drowned in a boat with which they were bringing sea-ware home, and being now alone she could not work her croft nor pay her rent. When everything was spent, and she had only one cow left of her fold of cattle, the factor came for the tax.

On reaching the township he took with him a carle, friendly to himself, to the widow's house, where the neighbours had gathered to ascertain the object of their visit. When the factor was told that the poor woman had no means to pay her rent, he asked if she had no cattle. She said that she had only one cow and that it was grazing at some distance from the house. He asked it to be brought where he was, and when he saw it he said, "It is a pity there are not more of the kind." Being the only one, it had got all the attention and was in good condition. She said she had no other. He said, "We will keep this one for the dues." It was taken away from the widow and put in a field that was surrounded by a stone wall, near the castle, along with the small red pony which the factor had with him. While he was in search of some one to drive it away, and taking his dinner in the carle's house, the young men of Duntulm climbed over the wall of the field, though high, and got out the animals, which they drove to the shore, where a boat was in readiness in which they were taken to the islet of Fladda *(Fladda 'chuain)*, two miles off. The men put them ashore there, and had their boat drawn up in Duntulm Bay before the factor and his companion returned to look for their property and found the park empty. On asking the men, who had again gathered, if they knew how the animals had escaped or where they were, they said there was no gap in the wall known to them, and that the only person likely to know of their whereabouts was a gifted woman who lived near the castle, in search of whom two of them went. They found her at home, on reaching the height where her house was, and told her all that had occurred, and how she was to go with them and say that the cattle had been charmed away to some wonderful place. Isabel said that she was not well prepared to go that day. The men asked what preparation she lacked *('dé an cion dòigh a bh' oirre)*. She then asked for one of the men's broad bonnets, and when she got it, rose, and leaving her hair, which was becoming grey, streaming over her shoulders, she put it on, and tying a goatskin round her, tying her shoes and making garters with stripes of the same fur, she put a rope of straw round her waist and took a large staff in her hand. "She is prepared at last, and come now," the men said. When she came in sight, the factor looked at her in amazement, for he had never before seen a creature of her appearance. Before she came near he called, "Wife, do you know where the horse and cow I put in the park are now?" She paid no attention to him, but kept on coming nearer *(cha do lag i air a ceum)*, till she stood at his shoulder. "To whom did the animals belong?" she asked him then. "The cow belonged to the king," he said, "and the horse to myself.' "How could a cow belonging to the king be in this township?" she asked. "This woman gave it to me for the tax," he said, pointing to the widow. "She did not give it to you; she said you took it with you; and it is now that I understand the meaning of what happened when I was in my own house to-day, and heard an uproar *(straighlich)* in the air above that was greater than any one could ever have heard, and on looking for the cause of it, there it was in a fire; and though all the fires that you ever saw were gathered together, they would not make one like it; and in the last of the fire *('an earball an teine)* I looked to see what there was, and what was there but a horse and cow, while there were as good as five thousand little men, the hill men *(muinntir nan cnoc)*, who were not larger than bottles, going on, on each side of the fire; and if you had as much knowledge of the dwellers of these hills as I have, you would not touch the widow's portion, but if you are anxious to get back the animals —there before you, is the hill where they are, and where you can go and seek them, and if you can, find them." The man, who was terrified by her appearance and words, kept looking at her *('g a feitheamh)* and always drawing a step further off. He went home without horse or cow, and however long he remained in the office he held, the fear of the wise woman, (*Iseabal N'ic Rao'uill*) and the fairies kept him from ever returning to Duntulm.   When he was out of sight of the township, the young men of Duntulm went to the islet where they left the animals, which they brought back and gave to the poor woman, who was then able to pay the tax.

FOLK TALES.

THE TWO BROTHERS.

A TALE OF ENCHANTMENT.

IN early times, long ago, *('an toiseach an t-saoghail, o chionn nan cian)*, it is said that the island of Mull was uninhabited except by a few families who were living, on the south side at Carsaig, in that part of the island known as the Ross of Mull. These families lived isolated from the rest of the world; none of them had ever seen any one from anywhere else there, and none of themselves had ever left the place. They had no boats, and they said the other islets and land that they were seeing opposite were other worlds. One day, then, they saw coming on the sea before them *(mu 'n comhair)* from the mainland a speck *(dùradan)*, and when it came near they compared it to a horse with a tree standing on its back, but when it came to the shore it was a boat made of wicker-work covered with hides, with one man in it, who had some drink with him, and a quantity of hazel nuts for food, On account of his boat being covered with hides[1], they named him "The cowhide man, *(am boicionnach)*. On landing, he told them how he had left home, out of curiosity to see other places, and that was the first place he was able to reach. He is said to have come from Ardencaple in the district of Lorn on the mainland *(Ard-nan-capull, 'an Lathurna.)* He stayed a long time with them, as they treated him kindly, being much pleased with him. He taught them new ways that were useful to them in their every-day life, and by his skill and knowledge promoted their welfare in many ways. On seeing that they were not utilizing the milk of their cows and goats by making cheese from it, he asked them the reason of this. They told him that they did not know what cheese was, as they had never heard of it nor seen it, and would like well to know how it was made. They had the art of making butter among them previous to his coming. He took in *Lus-buidhe-bealltainn*, (marsh marigold) and putting its stalks in the milk turned it to curds and whey. This is said to be the first cheese that was made in Mull. Some time, nearly a year after this, another boat, or, as they described it, a horse with a tree in its back, was seen coming in the same way. This one came ashore at Lochspelvie, further eastward, and had one man in it also, whom they named "The one in the skin coverings" (*an craicionnach*). He was brother to the one who came before, and had come in search of him. The two strangers and the natives were agreeing well together, and the brothers began to build a boat when they found wood abundant in Mull. When the boat was finished they named it "the six-oared boat" (*iùrach nan sia ràmh*), and when it was fitted up and made ready for sailing, the two brothers took a crew with them and set off in it, to go to one or other of the worlds (*na saoghalan eile*) that they were seeing before them, and reached Jura (*Diùra*), but the natives of the island would not let them land, as they had never seen a boat before. They stoned them away from the shore. They then went to Colonsay, but the Colonsay men (*na Colosaich*) were equally hard-hearted (*doirbh*). They attacked them, and tried to blind them by throwing sand about their eyes. It was then that they went on to the green (*lit.*, blue) island (*an t-eilean gorm*), the name by which Islay was then known, where they arrived at a more favourable time, no one being before them at the shore. They drew the boat up on the land, and went on to see if there were people to be found on the island or if they would meet with anyone who could direct them to a house. The first person they met was an old man who was watching cattle (*aig aire sreud*). He thought they belonged to the island, as no one was known to have ever come to or gone away from it. The first of the brothers who came, asked the old man to give him information about the place. The old man remarked, "How curious your speech is, if you were born in this island." He said, "No, I am not a native of this island." The old man said, "And if not, what has brought you here?" "The reason of my coming is, to ask what you can give, and give what I may." The old man then, as it was nightfall, kindled a fire, and they sat with him till daylight, when men and houses were to be seen. The Islay men were hospitable to the strangers, who remained a full year and built seven boats for them. The elder brother married a woman of the country, and after some time he thought of returning to Mull again. Having prepared his boat he set off, taking his wife and the others with him, and set his course northwards (*aghaidh a bhàta, tuath*). They had not gone far when a thick mist came on which darkened their world, and as they had no compass and could see no land, they drifted till the boat went in to a shore. This was the first appearance of land they saw since leaving the *Eilean Gorm*. A big man came down where they were—they never saw his equal for size—and he caught the fore part of the boat and drew it up above high water mark, with them all in it. He invited them to go to his house. They went with him and were made welcome. The daughter of the house, on being asked by the elder of the two brothers for a drink, brought a a two-hooped wooden dish full of milk, set it on the floor beside them and went away. One of the strangers rose to lift the dish and he could not. Then three of them rose, but it defied them to lift it. She came back, and finding the dish as she left it, said, "If you have quenched your thirst it is not awanting from the measure (*air a' mheasair*). The cowhide one replied, "We have not been accustomed to stoop like cattle (*cromadh mar bhà*) when we take a drink, and we could not lift the dish." At that she caught the wooden dish by the ear, in her left hand, and held the drink to them all. "Where have you come from," she said, "or where are you going?" "We came from the dark-blue sea-isle," he said, "and are going to the hilly isle *(do 'n eilean bheannach)*." "That is Mull," she said, "Mull of my love, Mull of little men *(Muile mo ghràidh, Muile nam fear beaga)*." They passed that night cheerfully together, and went to put off to sea next day; but when they tried to move the boat and get it afloat, they might as well attempt to move the Rhinns of Islay *(an Roinn Ileach)* they could not move it. The young wife who came with them from Islay said then, "I know where we are; we are in the green isle that is under spells *(fo gheasaibh)*, but I have a gift that will let us leave it," and she told those with her how her mother had at parting given her a cap, saying, "If you are ever in a strait, put it on, and you must at the same time bend your head to the ground as low as your feet seven times *(seachd uairean do shròn a bhualadh ri òrdaig do choise)*." She had the cap in her belt *('n a cneas)*, and she told them to sit in the boat and take the oars. She then stood in their midst, touched the cap, bent her head, and it went up to her breast *(an cneas)*; the next time it went up to her neck *(am muineal)*; the third time, to her chin, *(an smigead)*; then, as she bent her head, at the fourth time, it went up past her mouth to her nose; the next time, it reached her eyes, then her forehead, at last the top of her head, and the boat was off. The mist was still there. They asked the eldest brother in which direction they were to set their course. He told them to follow the flight of birds, as they went shorewards in the evening and would guide them to land. There is a saying about the home-coming of birds and fish, that "Birds of the universe go westward, and fish of the deep eastward *(Eòin an domhain, siar, 's iasg an domhain, sear)*." During the night, the younger brother, the one of skins, called out that there was a mound before them *(gu 'n robh tòrr rompa)*. His brother who was in the afterpart of the boat said, " Is it a tòrr without grass," and it has got the name of Torrens to the present day (*'se na tòrrain a theirear riu gus an là 'n diugh*). They reached Mull shore when it was day, and they ran-in the boat at a narrow strait that was like an opening in a dyke (*cachaileith ghàraidh*), and before they got them from the tholepins, the oars were broken. The place is still known as the narrow strait of broken oars (*Caolas-a'-bhristidh-ràmh*). They got on shore, and went home and told where they had been and what had happened to them.

The person, now above 70 years of age, from whom the above story was taken down almost word for word by the writer, said that he heard the story when he was a young man, and that the following story (that of the two sisters), was a continuation of it; the incidents of the story occurred during the absence of the two brothers from the place, and were told to them by the natives, in return for the story of their own adventures. The name Torquil, which occurs in this story, and the belief in witchcraft and occult power indicated, suggests that the colony in Mull came originally from Lochlin, or that the story belongs to a later period of history than that that of "The two brothers." The story is as follows :—

THE TWO SISTERS AND THE CURSE.

Two sisters were living in the same township on the south side of Mull. One of them who was known as Lovely *Mairearad*[2] had a fairy sweetheart, who came where she was, unknown to anyone, until one day she confided the secret to her sister, who was called Ailsa[3] (*Ealasaid*), and told her how she dearly loved her fairy sweetheart. "And now, sister," she said, "you will not tell any one." "No," her sister answered, "I will not tell any one; that story will as soon pass from my lips as it will from my knee *(o'm ghlùn)*"; but she did not keep her promise; she told the secret of the fairy sweetheart to others, and when he came again, he found that he was observed, and he went away and never returned, nor was he seen or heard of ever after by any one in the place.   When the lovely sister came to know this, she left her home and became a wanderer among the hills and hollows, and never afterwards came inside of a house door, to stand or sit down, while she lived.   Those who herded cattle *(ag uallach threud)* tried frequently to get near her and persuade her to return home, but they never succeeded further than to hear her crooning a melancholy song in which she told how her sister had been false to her, and that the wrong done to her would be avenged on the sister or her descendants, if a fairy *(neach sìth)* has power.   On hearing that Ailsa was married, she repeated, "Dun Ailsa is married and has a son Torquil, and the evil will be avenged on her or on him *(phòs, phòs Ealasaid Odhar,* &c.)."   What she hummed in her mournful song was :—

> My mother's place is deserted, empty and cold,
> My father, who loved me, is asleep in the tomb,
> Friendless and solitary I wander through the fields,
> Since there is none in the world of my kindred
> But a sister without pity.
> She asked, and I told, out of the fulness of my joy ;
> There was none nearer of kin to know my secret ;
> But I felt, and this brought the tears to my eyes,
>   *(lit.,* raindrip on my sight),
> That a story comes sooner from the lip than from the knee.

She was then heard to utter these wishes—

> May nothing on which you have set your expectations ever grow,
> Nor dew ever fall on your ground.
> May no smoke rise from your dwelling,
> In the depth of the hardest winter,
> May the worm be in your store,
> And the moth under the lid of your chests.
> If a fay-being has power,
> Revenge will be taken though it may be on your descendants.

Tha suidheag mo mhàthar gu fàs, falamh, fuar,
Tha m' athair 'thug luaidh dhomh 'n a shuain fo 'n lic.
Gun daoine gun duine na raoin tha mi 'siubhal,
'S gun 's an t-saoghal do 'm chuideachd
Ach piuthar gun iochd.
Dh' iarr ise 's thug mise do mheud mo thoil-inntinn ;
'S mi gun neach 'bu dìsle g' an innsinn mo rùn ;
Ach dh' fhairich mi sid 's thug e snidh' air mo léirsinn
Gur luaithe 'thig sgeul o 'n bheul na o 'n ghlùn.

An sin thuirt i na guidheachan so :—

" Na-na-chinn 's na-na-chuir thu t-ùidh,
'S na-na-shil an driùchd ad àilios,
'S na-na-rug ad bhothan smùid
Ann an dùlachd crùth an crios;
Gu 'n robh a' chnuimheag ann ad stòr
'S an leòmann fo bhòrd do chist' ;
Ma tha cumhachd aig neach sìth,
Dìolar ge b' ann air do shliochd."

Ailsa *(Ealasaid)* married, and had one son. In some way
her afflicted sister heard of this, and she then added to her
song—

Dun Ailsa has married,
And she has a son Torquil.
Brown-haired Torquil who can climb the headland
And bring the seal off the waves,
The sickle in your hand is sharp,
You will in two swaths reap a sheaf.

Phòs, phòs Ealasaid Odhar,
'S tha mac aice—Torcuil.
Torcuil donn 'dhìreadh sròin,
'S a bheireadh ròn bhàrr nan stuadh,
Bu sgaiteach do chorran 'n ad dhòrn
'S dheanadh tu dhà dhlòth an sguab.

Whatever gifts the brown-haired only child of her sister was
favoured with, besides others, he was a noted reaper, but this
gift proved fatal to him *(dh' fhòghainn e dha)*. When he grew
up to manhood, he could reap as much as seven men, and none
among them could compete with him. He was then told that

G

a strange woman was seen coming to the harvest fields in autumn, after the reapers had left, and that she would reap a field before daylight next morning, or any part of the ripe corn that the reapers could not finish that day, and in whatever field she began, she left the work of seven reapers, finished, after her. She was known as the Maiden of the Cairn *(Gruagach[6] a' chùirn),* from being seen to come out of a cairn over opposite. One evening then, brown-haired Torquil, who desired to see her at work, being later than usual of returning home, on looking back saw her beginning in his own field. He returned, and finding his sickle where he had put it away, he took it with him, and after her he went. He resolved to overtake her and began to reap the next furrow, saying, "You are a good reaper or I will overtake you;" but the harder he worked, the more he saw that instead of getting nearer to her, she was drawing further away from him, and he then called out to her,

"Maiden of the cairn, wait for me, wait for me." *('Ghruagach a' chùirn, fuirich rium, fuirich rium.)*

She said, answering him,

"Handsome brown-haired youth, overtake me, overtake me." *('Fhleasgaich a' chuil-duinn, beir orm, beir orm.)*

He was confident that he would overtake her, and went on after her till the moon was darkened by a cloud; he then called to her,

"'The moon is clouded *(lit.* smothered by a cloud), delay, delay." *(Tha 'ghealach air a mùchadh fo nèòil, fuirich rium, fuirich rium.)*

"I have no other light but her, overtake me, overtake me," she said.

He did not, nor could he, overtake her, and on seeing again how far she was in advance of him, he said, "I am weary with yesterday's reaping, wait for me, wait for me." She answered, "I ascended the round hill of steep summits *(màm cas nan leac),* overtake me, overtake me;" but he could not. He then said, "My sickle would be the better of being sharpened *(air a bhleath)*, wait for me, wait for me." She answered, "My sickle will not cut garlic, overtake me, overtake me." At this she reached the head of the furrow, finished reaping, and stood still where she was, waiting for him. When he reached the head of his own furrow, he caught the last handful of corn,[7] to keep it, as was the custom, it being the "Harvest Maiden" *(a' mhaighdean-bhuana)*, and stood with it in one hand and the sickle in the other. Looking at her steadily in the face, he said,

"You have put the old woman far from me, and it is not my displeasure you deserve." *(Chuir thu a' chailleach fada uam 's cha b' e mo ghruaim a thoill thu.)*[8]

She said,

"It is an evil thing early on Monday to reap the harvest maiden." *('S dona 'n ni (var., mì-shealbhach) moch Di-luain dol a bhuain maighdein.)*

On her saying this, he fell dead on the field and never more drew breath. The Maiden of the Cairn was never afterwards seen, nor heard of; and that was how the sister's wishes ended.

NOTES.

1.—Boats made of twigs and covered with hides, the hairy side of the skin being uppermost, could go long distances over rough seas.

2.—This name is sometimes rendered in English, Margaret. Erraid Isle *(Eilean earraid)* is in the Sound of Iona, south of Mull.

3.—The rock of Ailsa in the firth of Clyde is called in Gaelic *Creag Ealasaid*, and *Ealasaid a' chuain* (Ailsa of the sea). A round grey rock lying near the shore in Mannal, south side of Tiree, is called

Sgeir Ealasaid, the Ailsa rock. The name *Ealasaid* is in English also Elizabeth and Elspeth.

4.—*Odhar,* dun or grey, is applied to cattle ; as, *bò mhaol odhar,* a dun hornless cow ; *gabhar mhaol odhar,* a grey goat : it is sometimes used as an expresssion of contempt, as *creutair odhar,* a dun creature. The diminutive of *odhar, odhrag,* is a pet name for a cow.

5.—The words of the first four lines of "the wishes," are, as regards their form in the Gaelic text, almost unintelligible ; they merely represent the sounds uttered by the reciter, without being correct either in form or composition. The sounds belonging to the first line might, for instance, have been represented thus :—'*Na ana-chìnnt 's 'n a an-shocair dhuit d' ùidh :* perhaps the utterance was intentionally ambiguous.—(Ed.)

6.—*Gruagach,* the supernatural being, in this instance was said to be a woman ; but *gruagach* usually meant a chief. (See Vol. IV., Argyllshire series, p. 193.)

7.—There was a custom at one time, that the last handful of corn that was cut, and which finished the harvest, was taken home by the reaper, who was usually the youngest person in the family who could reap. The bunch was tastefully decorated and kept, at least till the following year, as the harvest maiden.

8.—It was also a custom in other times for old women to go about asking charity, and if infirm, they were carried about from house to house and villages, and whoever was last in a township to finish the reaping of his corn had to maintain one that year, and the same thing might happen to him the next year. When the run-rig system was common, the last furrow of corn was sometimes left standing as no one could be got to own it, through fear of having to keep the old woman for a year.

THE DARK, OR PITCH-PINE, DAUGHTER OF THE NORSE KING,

AND HOW SHE THINNED THE WOODS OF LOCHABER.

WHEN the Norsemen came, and their visits were frequent and numerous, to this country and these islands, to lay claim to and take possession of the land, the fame they gathered for themselves through their indulgence in every manner of cruel spoliation, and slaughter of the people wherever they landed, was that they were a bold, courageous, hardy, rough ("The Norsemen a rough band"), peremptory and unscrupulous race, and more than that, it was attributed to them that they practised witchcraft, charms, and enchantments, and had much of other unhallowed learning among them. The Norse King's eldest daughter was particularly noted for her knowledge of the "Black Art." There was no accident or mischance that befell friends, or destruction that overtook enemies, or any luck or good fortune that attended either friend or foe, but it was said that she was the cause of it, or had some hand in it. She was famed at home and abroad, far and wide, for her skill among cows and cattle, she was said to possess every variety of dairy knowledge in her father's kingdom. There was no charm or evil eye that fell on any living creature in the fold but she could dispel and avert, nor hurt nor injury they got but she could heal, nor dizziness nor fits into which they fell, from which she could not restore them, until it was said of her that the lowing of cattle, the incoherent cry of calves, and the rough cry of yearlings was to her the sweetest and most soothing music, and that she would answer the call of cattle, though she might be lost in the midst of the northern woods, and the cry

from the nethermost part of the farthest off quarter of the
universe. She knew the herb that had the property of taking
its qualities from milk, as well as she was acquainted with the
spells by which its virtues could be restored, and every charm
and invocation that was practised or then esteemed. The
flowers of the meadows and woods were as familiar to her as
the ridges of corn or a grain on straw, and there was not a leaf
on tree, bush, or shrub, with whose properties she was not
acquainted. Her father's kingdom was clothed with pine
wood, and was then as now famous for the fine quality of the
wood from which most of the wealth of the kingdom was
obtained.

One of those times when the Norsemen came to Scotland to
take possession of and sub-divide the land thus taken, they
observed that the pine wood of Lochaber was growing so fast,
and extending so far, that in time it might supersede the Black
Forests of Sweden. But on this occasion the northern forces
were driven back. On reaching home they reported the matter
to the king, and their opinion, that the increase of the wood
must be checked, otherwise his northern woods would be of
little esteem.

It occurred to the King to consult his daughter on the
matter, since she was learned, and to get knowledge from her
of the best method of thinning and destroying the Scottish
wood. She gave him the desired information, but said that
she must be the bearer of the method and must necessarily go
to Scotland herself. She obtained the King's permission and
made preparations for the journey.

From the gifts she possessed, neither sea nor land, air nor
earth could hinder her progress until she accomplished her
purpose. When she reached Lochaber the method she adopted
was to kindle a fire in the selvage of her dress, and she then
began to go through the woods, and as she could travel in the
clouds as well as on the ground, when she ascended and whirled

in the air, the sparks of fire that flew from her dress were blown hither and thither by the wind and set the woods on fire, until the whole country was almost in a blaze, and so darkened by the smoke, that one could hardly see before them; and, from being blackened more than any tree in the forest, by the smoke and soot of the fiery furnace which surrounded her, she was known and spoken of by the name of "Dark, or Pitch Pine." The people gathered to watch her, but from the rapidity of her ascent and the swiftness with which she descended, they could not grasp her any more than they could prevent her, and were at a loss what to do. At last, they sought instruction from a learned man in the place. He advised them to collect a herd of cattle in a fold, wherever she would stand still, and whenever she heard the lowing of the cattle she would descend, and when she was within gun-shot they were to fire at her with a silver bullet, when she would become a faggot of bones. They followed this advice and began to gather cattle and follow after her until the pinfold large and small was full set in the "Centre of Kintail." Whenever she heard the cry of the herd she descended and they aimed at her with the silver bullet, as the wise man told them to do, and she fell gently among them. Men lifted the remains and carried them to Lochaber, and to make sure that dead or alive she would do no more injury to them, they buried her in Achnacarry; and the person from whom the story was first heard nine years ago [1880] said that he could put his foot on the place where she was buried.

The Norse King was amazed at his daughter not returning, and at his not receiving any account from her. He sent abroad to get tidings of her. When the news of the disaster that happened to her was brought to him, he sent a boat and crew to bring her home, but the Lochaber women by their incantations destroyed those whom he sent. The boat was wrecked, and the men lost, at the entrance to Locheil. The next ships that came were not more successful.   The third time the King sent out his most powerful fleet.   What they did then was to send and try through spells to dry up the wells of the Fairy Hill of Iona.   The virtue of these wells was that wind, could be obtained from any desired quarter by emptying them, in the direction of the wind wished for.   When the ships were seen approaching, the wells began to be emptied, and before the last handful was flung out, the storm was so violent, and the ships so near, that the whole fleet was driven on the beach under the Fairy Hill, and the power and might of the Norsemen was broken and so much weakened that they did not return again to infest the land.

AN DUBH GHIUBHSACH, NIGHEAN RIGH LOCHLAINN,

AGUS MAR A CHRIONAICH I COILLE LOCHABAIR.

MAR thàinig na Lochlannaich an toiseach, 's bu bhitheanta sin, air feadh nan dùthchannan 's nan eileinean so, a thogail chòraichean 's a ghabhail sealbh air fearann, 's e an cliù a choisinn iad dhaibh féin, leis gu 'n robh iad ris a h-uile seòrsa léir-chreach 's milleadh air muinntir nan àiteachan a bha iad a' ruigheachd, gu 'n robh iad 'n an daoine dalma, misneachail, cruaidh-chridheach, borb.   "Lochlannaich, a' bhuidheann bhorb," neo-easmaileach, neo-thròcaireach 's a thuilleadh air sin, bha e air chur as an leth gu 'n robh buidseachd agus druidheachd 's iomadh eòlas toirmisgte eile 'n am measg.

Bha 'n nighean a bu sine aig Righ Lochlainn sònraichte

ainmeil air son na bh' aice de 'n " Sgoil Dubh." Cha robh sgiorradh no tubaist a thachaireadh do chàirdean, no sgrios a thigeadh air naimhdean, no math no rath a dh' éireadh do h-aon diù, nach robh e air a ràdhainn gur i b' aobhar-cinn dha, no gu 'n robh làmh thaobh-eiginn aice ann. Bha i aig an tigh 's uaithe fada 's farsuinn comharraichte air son sgil am measg cruidh 's feudail ; 's ann aice bha gach seòrsa eòlas cruidh 'an rìoghachd a h-athar. Cha robh sian no sùil a laidheadh air creutair beo 's a' bhuaile nach togadh i, no tuaineal no ceangal 's an rachadh iad nach fhuasgladh i, gus an abairteadh gur e geumnaich cruidh, blaomannaich laogh agus ràcaireachd ghamhna an t-aon cheòl cadail a bu bhinn leatha, 's gu 'm freagradh i 'n uair a chluinneadh i 'n spréidh ged bhiodh i 'n a suain an teis-meadhon coille dhubh a h-athar 's an geum o cheann ìochdar iomall an domhain.

B' aithne dh' i an lus a bheireadh an toradh as a' bhainne co math 's a b' aithne dh' i na h-eòlais a thilleadh air ais e, agus gach seòrsa sian agus oradh a bha air a chleachdainn no air a chunntas feumail 's an àm. Bha gach luibh 's a' mhachair no 's a' choille co-ionnan dh' i ri arbhar nan imirean no spilgean cònlaich, 's cha robh duilleag air craoibh, no preas, no dris, nach b' aithne dh' i. 'S an àm so bha dùthaich a h-athar còmh-daichte le coille ghiubhais, agus iomraideach (mar tha fhathast) air son co math 's a bha a fiodh, 's bha neart de bheartais na rìoghachd 'tighinn a stigh air a tailibh.

· Uair de na h-uairean sin thàinig na Lochlannaich do Albainn a thoirt a mach fearainn 's a dheanamh roinn na còrach air na gheibheadh iad, 's thug iad fainear gu 'n robh coille ghiubhais Lochabair a' fàs 's a' gabhail roimpe co mòr 's gu 'm faodtadh e 'bhi gu 'n cuireadh i stad air coille dhubh na Suain. Chaidh feachd Lochlannach an uair so thilleadh air ais an taobh a thàinig iad, 's 'n uair a ràinig iad dhachaidh dh' innis iad do 'n righ mar bha iad 'am beachd a thachradh 's gu 'm feumadh stad a chur air cinneas na coille Albanaich neo nach bitheadh mòran

meas air a' chonnadh aige-san. 'S e smuaintich an righ bho 'n
a bha h-uile ionnsachadh aig a nighean gu 'n cuireadh e 'chomhairle rithe, 's gu 'm faigheadh e fiosrachadh uaipe 'd e an dòigh
a b' fhearr 's a bu luaithe air a' choille Albanaich a dheanamh
na bu lugha 's a crìonadh. Dh' innis i dha, ach gu 'm bitheadh
aice fhéin ri dol ann. Fhuair i cead o 'n Rìgh, 's rinn i deas
air son falbh; 's leis na cumhachdan a bh' aice cha chuireadh
muir no tìr, talamh no adhar, stad air a ceum gus an ruigeadh
i ceann thall a' ghnothaich.

'N uair a ràinig i Lochabair 's e 'n dòigh a ghabh i, dh'
fhadaidh i teine 'an iomall a gùin 's ghabh i gu siubhal roimh
'n choille, 's leis gu robh comas aice falbh anns na neòil co
math 's air an talamh, dhìreadh i suas agus 'n uair bha i 'dìreadh
's a' cur cuairteig anns an adhar, bha na sradagan teine a bha
'falbh as a gùn a' dol gach taobh leis a' ghaoith 's a' lasadh na
coille gus an robh an dùthaich uile gu bhi 'n a caoirean teintich
's co dùinte le deathaich 's gur gann a bu léir do dhuine lias, 's a
chionn gu 'n robh i fhéin air fàs anns an deathaich 's anns an
t-sùith na bu duibhe na craobh 's a' choille, 's e "An Dubh
Ghiùbhsach" a theireadh iad rithe.

Bha muinntir na dùthcha cruinn còmhla 'g a feitheamh 's cha
chumadh iad sealladh oirre leis co àrd 's a rachadh i anns na
speuran 's co luath 's a thèarnadh i gu talamh. Cha b' urrainn
iad greim fhaighinn oirre na bu mhotha na b' urrainn iad stad
a chur oirre, 's cha robh fios aca 'd e a dhèanadh iad. Mu
dheireadh chaidh iad air son fòghluim gu duine ionnsaichte a
bha 's an dùthaich. Thuirt esan riu, buaile cruidh a chruinn-
eachadh far an stadadh i, 's 'n uair a chluinneadh i 'n fheudail
's a' bhuar gu 'n tèarnadh i; 's an uair a bhiodh i mar urchair
gunna uapa iad a losgadh oirre le peileir airgid, 's gu 'n rachadh i 'n a cual chnàmh. Ghabh iad a chomhairle 's thòisich
iad air togail chreach 's air ise leantuinn gus an robh a' bhuaile
làn-suidhichte le crodh ann an Crò-Chintàile. Co luath 's a
chuala ise a' gheumnaich theirinn i 's loisg iad oirre leis a'

pheileir airgid mar dh'iarr an duine glic orra, 's thuit i 'n a
ceòsaich 'n am measg. Thog iad eadar dhaoine am pronnan a
bh' aca dhi 's thug iad leo do Lochabair i, 's chum gu 'm bitheadh iad cinnteach nach dèanadh i cron beò no marbh dhoibh
tuilleadh, thìodhlaic iad i ann an Achanacairidh ; 's am fear
bho 'n deachaidh an naigheachd a chluinntinn an toiseach—
anns a' bhliadhna 1880—bha e 'g ràdhainn gu 'm b' urrainn dha
a chas a chur air an uaigh anns an do chuireadh i.

Bha ioghnadh air Righ Lochlainn nach robh a nighean a'
tilleadh no sgeul uaipe. Chuir e forfhais a mach, 's trà chualaic
e mar thachair dhi, chuir e bàta 's sgioba air son a toirt dachaidh, ach dh' fhoghain mnathan Lochabair le 'n ubagan dh' i.
Chaidh a briste 's na daoine chall, aig bun Lochiall. Cha d'
ràinig an ath chabhlach na bu mhò. 'S an treasa uair trà chuir
an Righ mach feachd na rioghachd 's e rinn iadsan, chuir iad
eòlas a thaomadh tobraichean Dhun-I, 's bha e 'n cois an eòlais,
rathad 's am bith a rachadh na tobraichean a thaomadh gu 'm
faighteadh a' ghaoth a dh' iarrtadh. 'N uair fhuaradh scalladh
air a' chabhlach, thòisichear air taomadh an tobair, 's mu 'n robh
a' bhoiseag mu dheireadh as, bha a' ghaoth co làidir 's a' chabhlach co dlùth 's gu 'n do bhrisdeadh iad air cladach an Dùin,
's chaidh cumhachd 's feachd nan Lochlannach lughdachadh co
mòr 's nach do thill iad riamh tuilleadh a dheanamh dòlais no
a thoirt sgrios air an tir.

THERE was a smith, before now, in Ireland, who was one day working in the smithy, when a youth came in, having two old women with him.

He said to the smith,

"I would be obliged to you," he said, "if you would let me have a while at the bellows and anvil."

The smith said he would. He then caught the two old women, threw a hoop about their middle, and placed them in the smithy fire, and blew the bellows at them, and then took them out and made one woman, the fairest that eye ever saw, from the two old women.

When the smith laid down at night, he said to his wife,

"A man came the way of the smithy to-day, having with him two old women; he asked from me a while of the bellows and anvil, and he made the fairest woman that man's eye ever saw, out of the two old women. My own mother and your mother are here with us, and I think I will try to make one right woman of the two since I saw the other man doing it."

"Do," she said, "I am quite willing."

Next day he took out the two old women, put the hoop about their middle, and threw them in the smithy fire. It was not long before it became likely that he would not have even the bones of them left. The smith was in extremity, not knowing what to do, but a voice came behind him,

"You are perplexed, smith, but perhaps I will put you right." With that he caught the bellows and blew harder at them; he then took them out and put them on the anvil, and made as fair a woman out of the two old wives. Then he said to the smith,

"You had need of me to-day, but," said he, "you better engage me; I will not ask from you but the half of what I earn, and that this will be in the agreement, that I shall have the third of my own will." The smith engaged him.

At this time O'Neil sent abroad word that he wanted one who would make the hair of his head to grow, for there was none on the head of O'Neil or O'Donnell, his brother, and that whoever could do it, would get the fourth part of his means. The servant lad said to the smith,

"We had better go and make a bargain with O'Neil that we will put hair on his head," and they did this. "Say you to him," said the servant lad, "that you have a servant who will put hair on his head for the fourth part of what he possesses."

O'Neil was agreeable to this, and the servant lad desired to get a room for themselves, and asked a cauldron to be put on a good fire. It was done as he wished. O'Neil was taken in and stretched on a table. The servant lad then took hold of the axe, threw off O'Neil's head, and put it face foremost in the cauldron. After some time he took hold of a large prong which he had, and he lifted up the head with it, and hair was beginning to come upon it. In a while he lifted it up again with the same prong, this time a ply of the fine yellow hair would go round his hand. Then he gave the head such a lift, and stuck it on the body. O'Neil then called out to him to make haste and let him rise to his feet, when he saw the fine yellow hair coming in into his eyes. He did as he had promised; he gave the smith and the servant lad the fourth part of his possessions. When they were going home with the cattle the servant lad said to the smith,

"We are now going to separate, we will make two halves or divisions of the cattle."

The smith was not willing to agree to this, but since it was in his bargain he got the one half. They then parted, and the animal the smith would not lose now, he would lose again, he did not know where he was going before he reached home, and he had only one old cow that he did not lose of the cattle.

When O'Donnell saw his brother's hair, he sent out word that he would give the third part of his property to any one who would do the same to himself. The smith thought he would try to do it this time alone. He went where O'Donnell was, and said to him that he would put hair on his head for him also, as he had done to his brother O'Neil. Then he asked that the cauldron be put on, and a good fire below it, and he took O'Donnell into a room, tied him on a table, then took up an axe, cut off his head, and threw it, face downwards, into the cauldron. In a while he took the prong to see if the hair was growing, but instead of the hair growing, the jaws were nearly falling out. The smith was almost out of his senses, not knowing what to do, when he heard a voice behind him saying to him, "You are in a strait." This was the lad with the Black Art, he formerly had, returned. He blew at the cauldron stronger, brought the prong to see how the head was doing, or if the hair was growing on it. The next time he tried it, it would twine round his hand. Since it was so long of growing on it, he said, "We will put an additional fold round my hand." When he tried it again it would reach two twists. He took it out of the cauldron and stuck it on the body. It cried to be quickly let go, when he saw his yellow hair down on his shoulders. The hair pleased him greatly; it was more abundant than that of O'Neil, his brother. They got fully what was promised them, and were going on their way home. The lad who had the Black Art said, "Had we not better divide the cattle?"

"We will not, we will not," said the smith, "lift them with you, since I got clear."

"Well," said the other, "if you had said that before, you

would not have gone home empty-handed, or with only one cow," and with that he said, "You will take every one of them: I will take none of them."

The smith went home with that herd, and he did not require to strike a blow in his smithy, neither did he meet with the one with the Black Art, ever after.

O' NEIL, 'S MAR A CHAIDH AM FALT AIR A CHEANN.

GOBHAINN bh' ann roimhe so ann an Eirinn, 's bha e latha de na làithean ag obair anns a' cheàrdaich agus thàinig òganach stigh 's dà sheana-bhoirionnach aige. Thuirt e ris a' ghobhainn, "Bhithinn ann ad chomain," ars' esan, "na 'n toireadh tu dhomh tacan de 'n bholg 's de 'n innean." Thuirt an gobhainn ris gu 'n tugadh. Rug e an sin air an dà chaillich, chaith e cearcall mu 'm meadhon, 's chàirich e 's an teallach iad, 's shéid e am bolg riu ; thug e 'n sin mach iad 's rinn e aon bhoirionn-ach a bu bhreadha 's a chunnaic sùil duine de 'n dà chaillich. 'N uair a luidh an gobhainn 's an oidhche, thuirt e ris a mhnaoi, "Thàinig fear rathad na ceàrdaich an diugh 's dà chaillich aige, 's dh' iarr e orm treis de 'n bholg 's de 'n innean, 's rinn e 'm boirionnach a bu bhriadha a chunnaic sùil duine riamh air an

dà chaillich. Tha mo mhàthair fhéin 's do mhàthair fhéin
againn ann an so, 's tha mi 'smaointeachadh gu 'm feuch mi ri
aon bhoirionnach ceart a dheanamh orra bho 'n a chunnaic mi
am fear eile 'g a dheanamh."

"Dean," ars' ise, "tha mi làn-toileach."

Am màireach thug e mach an dà chaillich 's chuir e 'n cearcall
mu 'm meadhon, 's thilg e 's an teallach iad. Cha b' fhada ach
gus an robh coltach nach bitheadh na cnàimhean fhéin aige
dhiùbh. Bha an gobhainn 'n a chàs gun fhios aige 'dé dheanadh e, ach thàinig guth air a chùlthaobh, "Tha thu ann ad
éiginn, a ghobhainn, ach ma dh' fhaoidte gu 'n cuir mise ceart
thu." Rug e air a' bholg 's théid e na 's teinne riu; thug e
mach iad a sin 's chuir e air an innean iad, 's rinn e boirionnach
a bu bhriadha de 'n dà chaillich. Thuirt e sin ris a' ghobhainn,
"Bha feum agad ormsa an diugh, ach," ars' esan, "'s ann a 's
fearr dhuit mise fhasdadh, 's cha 'n iarr mi ort ach darna leth
de na bheir mi a mach; ach gu 'm bi so anns a' chùmhnant,
gu 'm bi an treas trian de m' thoil fhéin agam." Dh' fhasdaidh
an gobhainn e.

Aig an àm sin chuir O' Neil mach fios na 'm faigheadh e fear
a chuireadh falt air, chionn cha robh falt idir air O' Neil na
air O' Domhnull a bhràthair, gu 'n toireadh e dhoibh a' cheathramh chuid d' a mhaoin; 's thuirt an gille ris a' ghobhainn,
"'S fhearr dhuinne falbh 's bargan a dheanamh ri O' Neil gu 'n
cuir sinn falt air;" 's rinn iad mar sin. "Abair thusa ris,"
thuirt an gille ris a' ghobhainn, "gu bheil gille agadsa a chuir-
eas falt air, air son a' cheathramh chuid d' a mhaoin."

Bha O' Neil deònach air a shon so, agus dh' iarr an gille
seòmar fhaotainn dhoibh fhéin, 's dh' iarr e coire a chur air, 's
teine math ris. Rinneadh mar a dh' iarr e, 's chaidh O' Neil a
thoirt stigh, 's chuir e 'n a shìneadh air bòrd e, 's rug e air an
tuaidh 's thilg e dheth an ceann, 's chuir e 'n comhair na goille
anns a' choire e. 'An ceann tacain rug e air gramaiche mòr a
bh' aige 's thog e suas an ceann leis, 's bha toiseach fuilt a' tigh-

inn air. Ann an ceann treis thog e suas a rithist e leis a' ghramaiche cheudna, agus an uair so ruigeadh car m' a dhòrn de 'n
fhalt bhriadha bhuidhe. Thug e sin an togail ud air, 's bhuail
e air a' choluinn e. Ghlaodh sin O' Neil greasad air 's a leigeil
air a chois, 'n uair a chunnaic e 'm falt briadha buidhe a' tighinn 'n a shùilean. Rinn e riu mar a gheall e; fhuair iad a
cheathramh chuid d' a mhaoin.

'N uair bha iad so 'dol dachaidh 's an spréidh aca, thuirt an
gille ris a' ghobhainn, "Tha mi nis 'dol a dhealachadh ribh,
's nì sinn dà leth air an spréidh." Cha robh an gobhainn toil-
each air so a thoirt dha, ach bho 'n a bha e 'n a chùmhnant
fhuair e 'n darna leth. Dhealaich iad so, agus am beothach
nach cailleadh an gobhainn an dràsd' shiubhladh e rithist, 's cha
robh fhios aige c' àite an robh e a' dol, 's mu 'n d' ràinig e 'n
tigh cha robh aige ach seann mhart nach do chaill e de 'n
spréidh

'N uair a chunnaic O' Domhnull am falt a bh' air a bhràthair,
chuir e mach fios gu 'n toireadh e 'n treas cuid d' a mhaoin
seachad do aon 's am bith a chuireadh air fhéin e. Smaointich
an gobhainn gu 'm feuchadh e-fhéin g' a dheanamh an dràsda
gun duine ach e-fhéin. Chaidh e far an robh O'Domhnull 's
thuirt e ris gu 'n cuireadh e air-san e mar an ceudna, 's gur e
a chuir air a bhràthair, O'Neil, e, 's dh' iarr e 'n coire 'chur air
's teine math ris. Thug e O' Domhnull stigh do sheòmar 's
cheangail e air bòrd e, 's rug e air an tuaidh, 's thug e dheth an
ceann 's thilg e 'an comhair na goille e anns a' choire. 'An
ceann treis rug e air a' ghramaiche dh' fheuchainn an robh falt
a' cinntinn, ach 'an àite falt a bhi 'cinntinn 's ann a bha na
giallan 'tuiteam as. Bha an gobhainn 'an impis dol as a chiall,
gun fhios aige 'dé dheanadh e, 'n uair a chualaig e guth air a
chùlthaobh ag ràdhainn ris, "Tha thu ann ad éiginn." Bha so
gille na sgoil-duibhe, a bh' aige fhéin roimhe, air tilleadh.
Shéid e ris a' choire na bu teodha, 's thug e sin nuas leis an
gramaiche a shealltainn ciamar a bha an ceann a' deanamh, 's

H

bha am falt a' cinntinn. An ath-uair a dh' fheuch e e, ruigeadh car mu 'dhòrn dheth. "Bho 'n a bha e co fada gun chinntinn," ars' esan, "cuiridh sinn car a bharrachd mu 'm dhòrn;" 's 'n uair a dh' fheuch e rithist e, ruigeadh e 'n dà char. Thog e as a' choire e, 's bhuail e air a' choluinn e; 's ghlaodh e 'ghrad-fhuasgladh, 's e 'faicinn 'fhalt buidhe sìos air a ghualainn. Chòrd am falt ris fìor mhaith, bha barrachd fuilt air 's a bh' air O' Neil a bhràthair. Fhuair iadsan 'cheart ni a chaidh ghealltainn doibh, 's bha iad 'dol dachaidh air an rathad. Thuirt gille na sgoil-duibhe, "Nach fheàrr dhuinn ar treud a roinn?" "Cha roinn, cha roinn," ars' an gobhainn, "tog leat iad, bho 'n a fhuair mise saor." "Ma tà," ars' esan, "na 'n dubhairt thu sin roimhe cha deachaidh thu dhachaidh falamh no air aon mhart; agus leis a sin," ars' esan, "bheir thu leat h-uile h-aon diùbh, cha ghabh mise gin diùbh."

Chaidh an gobhainn dachaidh leis an spréidh sin, 's cha do ruig e leas buille a bhualadh 'an ceàrdaich tuille, ni mò a thachair e-fhéin air fear na sgoil-duibhe tuille.

BEAST FABLES.

Aarne 1

W.H.T. III

THE WOLF AND THE FOX.

THIS story, like many others in which the lower animals figure as characters, is very popular in the Highlands, in fact, Mr. Campbell of Islay, by whom it is mentioned, could not help falling in with it. But the version published by him is destitute of several interesting incidents which form a part of the story. The narration depends always upon the knowledge and skill of the person who tells it, and this edition is given because there is to be found in it incidents of much interest and amusement, not to be found in any other version, such as the Fox's oath and standing in front of the fire. The Gaelic is not given except in the essential expressions, and it is not deemed of much consequence to give more, as their fluency and number depend upon the reciter's knowledge and tact. In these fables the lower animals appear with the same characteristics as are always assigned to them, and in this tale the fox appears as not only wily and cunning, but also as the most unprincipled scoundrel, indifferent to the interests of others, and also to what is usually of weight with men, the restraint of an nnseen power.

The Fox and Wolf were keeping house together near the shore, and as might naturally be expected, were very poor and at times hard up for food. At first the fox kept himself in good condition, and was not so voracious as the wolf. After a heavy storm in winter time the two went along the shore to see what the sea had cast up. This is still done by poor people in the islands, and in those places where wood does not grow. They are often fortunate enough to find logs and planks of wood. On the occasion of the wolf and the fox's journey they were fortunate enough to find a keg of butter. Probably it had come from Ireland and been swept or thrown overboard in the storm. It was particularly welcome to the poor finders, and the rascally fox at once coveted it for himself. He said to the wolf that, as this was the winter time, they had not so much need of it, but when the hungry summer *(samhradh gortach)* would come, it would be doubly welcome ; they had better bury it, and no one would know of its existence but themselves. They dug a deep hole, buried the keg of butter, and went home with their other provisions. Some days after that the fox came in, and wearily throwing himself on a settle, or seat, which formed part of the furniture, he heaved a deep sigh and said, "Alas! Alas! Woe is me *(Och! Och! fhéin thall)*."

"Alas! Alas!" said the sympathising wolf, "what is it that troubles you ?"

"Dear me," said the fox, "they are wanting me out to a christening *(Och! Och! tha iad 'gam iarraidh mach gu goisteachd)*," still pretending a weary indifference, and the Gaelic expression is here noticeable, as, being asked out to a baptism means literally being asked to be god-father, or gossip at the baptism, a practise observed in the Highlands, even where the Roman Catholic and Episcopal systems have disappeared.

"Alas! Alas!" said the wolf, "are you going ?"

"Alas! Alas!" said the fox, "I am." When he came home, the wolf asked what name they had given the child. "A queer enough name," said the fox, " *Blaiseam*," (let me taste).

Some days after that again the same manœuvre was gone through, and when the fox returned and the wolf asked him the child's name, he said it was as queer a name as the former one,—" *Bi 'na mheadhon*," (be in its middle). A third time the manœuvre was gone through and the child's name was said to be the queerest of all, "*Sgrìob an clàr*," (scrape the stave).

At last the "hungry summer" came; and it was such as is well known even in eastern countries when the stores of the preceding harvest are exhausted, and the stores of the year's harvest are not yet ready. The fox and the wolf went for the keg of butter, but it had disappeared. The fox being prepared for this emergency began at once to accuse the wolf of having taken it, "No one knew it was there but our two selves, and I see the colour of it on your fur."

The two went away home, the wolf very much cast down, and the fox persisting in his accusation that the wolf had stolen it. The wolf solemnly protested that he had never touched it.

"Will you swear then?" the fox said.

According to a Highland proverb, protestations may be loud till they are solemn oaths (*'S mòr facal gu lùghadh*). The wolf then held up its paw, and with great solemnity emitted this oath, "If it be that I stole the butter, and it be, and it be, may disease lie heavy on my grey belly in the dust, in the dust," (*Ma 's mise ghoid an t-ìm, 's gur mi, 's gur mi, Galar trom-ghlas air mo bhronnghlas anns an ùir, anns an ùir*).

"Swear now yourself," but the fox was so impressed by the dignity and reverence of the oath, that he tried every means in his power to evade so solemn an ordeal; but the wolf would take no refusal, and at last the fox emitted this oath, "If it be I that stole the butter, and it be, and it be, Whirm, Wheeckam, Whirram, Whycam Whirrim Whew, Whirrim Whew," (*Ma's mise 'ghoid an t-ìm 's gur a mi, 's gur a mi, cìream, clceam cìream cuaigeam, cìream ciu, cìream ciu*). The student of language will observe how the Gaelic C corresponds to the English Wh. This is particularly noticeable here as the difference renders the oath as ludicrous in the translation as in the original, if not more so. The wolf said nothing, but the fox, with that persistence which often accompanies evil-doing, suggested that they should both stand in front of the fire and whoever began to sweat first would be the guilty party, as the butter would be oozing out

Γ. Ι
No 19

through him.   The wolf thinking no evil, consented, and the fox thought he would get him to stand nearer to the fire than himself.   It so turned out however, that the fox, who had kept himself in good condition by repeated visits to the keg of butter, (and they must have been more frequent than the baptisms to which he said he had been called), was getting uncomfortably warm, and said, "We are long enough at this work, we had better go out and take a walk."   When out thus cooling themselves, they passed a smithy door, at which an old white horse was standing with the point of its hind shoe resting on the ground.   The wolf having gone over to it, but at a safe distance, and looking intently at the door, said to the fox, "I wish, as your eyesight is better than mine and you can read better than I can, that you would come over and read the name written on the horse shoe.

The fox came over but could see no writing on the shoe, but flattered by the wolf's words, and not liking to confess that his eyesight was failing, it went closer and the horse lifting its foot knocked its brains out.

"I see," said the wolf, "the greatest scholars are not always the wisest clerks," *(Cha 'n i an ro-sgoilearachd a 's fhearr.—* *Lit.*—Excessive scholarship is not always the best.

THE FOX AND THE BIRD.

In the foregoing the fox appears true to his character as an unscrupulous, grasping, wily wretch, and in the following he appears as over reached by a bird. Considering the character the fox bears, one is glad when he is paid back in his own coin. The bird in the tale is by some rendered Kestrel Hawk, and by others Hen Harrier. The story was heard in Tiree, in which are no trees on which the bird could sit, and no hawks or foxes to make the story applicable. The lesson which the fable im- plies is one that is useful everywhere.

A *Deargan-allt, Eun Fionn*, was dosing by a river side, when a Fox came and caught it, and was going to devour it. "Oh don't, don't," said the bird, "and I will lay an egg as big as your head."

He protested this so loudly, and so solemnly, that the fox loosened his hold till the bird at last flew up into a tree. Here sitting on a branch, and safe from further injury, it said to the fox, " I will not lay an egg as big as your head, for I cannot do it, but I will give you three pieces of advice, and if you will observe them, they will do you more good in the future. One, first, "Never believe an unlikely story from unreliable authority *(Na creid naigheachd mi-choltach fo urrainn mi-dhealbhach)*. Secondly, "Never make a great fuss about a small matter *(Na dean dearmail mhòr mu rud beag)*, and thirdly"—here the bird seemed to take time, and the fox having his curiosity now excited listened, though it was with firmly clasped teeth and pangs of hunger—"Whatever you get a hold of, take a firm hold of it " *(Rud air an dean thu greim, dean greim gu ro-mhath air)*, saying this, the bird flew away, and the fox, thus neatly sold, was left lamenting.

In the Fables relating to animals the fox readily takes a lead, and is characterised as an unscrupulous and unprincipled rascal. Next to him the wren, which is the smallest (or at least has the name of being so) of British birds figures, and has got the name not only of being small, but also of being forward and pert. The first or most prominent of these fables is that in which the wren appears as contesting with the eagle the supremacy among birds, and this story may be said to be as widely extended over the Highlands as the birds themselves. There was to be a contest which bird should fly highest, and the wren jumped upon the eagle's back. When the eagle had soared as high as it could, it said, "Where are you now, brown wren?" (*C' àite bheil thu, dhreathan donn?*). The wren jumped up a little higher and said, "Far, far, above you" (*Fada fada fos do chionn*). In consequence of this extraordinary feat the wren has twelve eggs while the eagle has only two.

Natural historians assert that the number of wren's eggs in one nest seldom exceed eight, but others have stated that the most number is twelve or even fourteen. In these tales which have been got together in the West Highlands, the number is uniformly said to be twelve, but whether this is actually the case or merely an assumption, there is no call here for enquiring.

The wren and his twelve sons were threshing corn in a barn, when a fox entered and claimed one of the workers for his prize. It was agreed, since he must get some one, that it should be the old wren, if he himself could point him out from the rest. The thirteen wrens were so much alike that the fox was puzzled. At last he said, "It is easy to distinguish the stroke of the old hero himself" (*'S fhurasda buille an t-sean laoich aithneachadh*). On hearing this, the old wren gave himself a jauntier air, and said, "there was a day when such was the case" (*Bha latha dha sin*). After this the fox had no difficulty, for boasting was always illfated (*bha tubaist air a' bhòsd riamh*) and he took his victim without any dispute.

On another occasion the wren and his twelve sons were going to the peatmoss, when they fell in with a plant of great virtue and high esteem. The old wren caught hold of the plant by the ears, and was jerking it this way and that way, hard-binding it, and pulling it, as if peat-slicing; white was his face and red his cheek, but he failed to pull the plant from the bare surface of the earth: the plant of virtues and blessings— (*Bha e 'ga dhudadh null 's 'ga dhudadh nall, 'ga-chruaidh-cheangal 's 'ga bhuain-mòine; bu gheal a shnuadh 's bu dhearg a ghruaidh, 's cha tugadh e Meacain o chraicionn loma na talmhain; Meacan nam buadh 's nam beannachd*).

The wren called for the assistance of one of his sons, saying, "Over here one of my sons to help me" (*An so aon eallach mo mhac nall*), and they caught the plant in the same way, jerking it this way and that way, hard-binding and peat-slicing with it; white were their faces and red their cheeks, but they could not with all their ardour, and their utmost strength pull the plant from the bare surface of the earth: the plant of virtues and blessings (*'S bha iad 'ga dhudadh null 's 'ga dhudadh nall, 'ga chruaidh-cheangal 's 'ga bhuain-mòine; bu gheal an snuadh 's bu dearg an gruaidh ach le 'n uile dhichioll 's le 'n cruaidh-neart cha tugadh iad am Meacan o chraicionn loma na talmhain: Meacan nam buadh 's nam beannachd*).

"Over here with two of my sons to help me" (*An so dà eallach mo mhac nall*), and the same operation was again performed unsuccessfully, and in the same way one after another, until the whole twelve sons came to the assistance of the old wren. Then they grasped it altogether, and under the severe strain the plant at last yielded, and all the wrens fell backwards into a peat pond and were drowned.

The old man from whom this story was heard said, that in winter time, when knitting straw ropes for thatching, he could get all the boys of the village to come to assist him, and keep him company, and this they did with cheerfulness on the understanding that the story of "The wren and his twelve sons" would be illustrated at the end. One after another of the boys sat on the floor behind him, and he having a hold of the straw rope was able easily to resist the strain till he choose to let go, then all the boys fell back and the laughter that ensured was ample reward for their labour.

The fame of the wren for its forwardness and impudence is also illustrated by a story current in the south of Scotland, about Robin Redbreast having fallen sick, and the wren paying him a visit, and expressing great condolence when, after making his will, Robin dismissed her, saying, "Gae pack oot at my chamber door, ye cuttie quean." In Gaelic the wren is also known by the name of *Dreòllan*, and *Dreathan-donn*, and the the name as applied to human beings means a weakly, imbecile, trifling person, in whatever he takes in hand to do.

All the other birds in the same manner have their own share of actions ascribed to them, and the manner in which several of them made a brag of their own young is amusing—particularly in Gaelic, in which the call ascribed to them is more capable of imitation, and particularly in the light of the manner in which the young of those who make the boast are looked upon.

"Gleeful, gleeful," said the Gull, "my young is the supreme beauty."

"Sorry, sorry," said the Hooded Crow, "but my son is the little Blue Chick."

"Croak, croak," said the Raven, "it is my son that can pick the lambs."

"Click, click," said the Eagle, "it is my son that is lord over you."

("Glîtheag, glitheag," ors an Fhaoilean, "'se mo mhac-sa an Daogheal Donn."

"Gurra, gurra," thuirt an Fheannag, "'se mo mo mhac-sa an Garrach Gorm."

"Gnog, gnog," ors am Fitheach, "'s e mo mhac-sa 'chriomas na h-uain."

"Glig, glig," thuirt an Iolaire, "'s e mo mhac-sa 's tighearna oirbh.")

In the Highlands the young gull is called *Sgliùrach* which is the regular name for a slatternly young woman. It is seen in the midst of a storm alighting in the hollows, and restfully gliding to the highest summits of the waves.

The hooded crow's fancy for its own young has passed into a proverb, "The hooded crow thinks its own impertinent blue progeny pretty" *('S bòidheach leis an fheannaig a garrach gorm fhein").*

Of the Raven it is commonly said, that it is so fond of its victim's eyes that it will not even give them to its own young. Its supernatural knowledge of where carrion is to be found amounts almost to instinct, and is among the vices *(Dubhailcean)* ascribed to the bard.

The eagle can only fly from an elevated situation, from the difficulty of getting wind under its wings, and in this respect forms a great contrast to the little wren.

Of other tales in which the lower animals figure, the three following are noticeable.

I.—THE TWO DEER. The young, confident of its own speed and strength, remarked :—

> "Sleek and yellow is my skin,
> And no beast ever planted foot
> On hillside that could catch me."

The old deer, who knew better, answered,

> " The young dog black-mouthed
> And yellow : the first dog

Of the first litter.   Born in March,
And fed on quern meal and goat's milk,
There never planted foot on hillside
Beast it could not catch."

(Sleamhuinn 's buidhe mo bhian,
'S cha do chuir e eang air sliabh
Beathach riamh 'bheireadh orm."

"An cuilean bus-dubh buidhe,
Ceud chù na saighe
Rugadh anns a' Mhàrt
'S a bheathaichte air gairbhean
'S air bainne ghabhair
Cha do chuir e eang air sliabh
Beathach riamh nach beireadh e air).

Regarding this description of the deer-hound it deserves
notice that the word *Màrt*, translated March, denotes any busy
time of the year, there being a *màrt*, or busy season in harvest
as well as in spring, *Màrt Fogharaidh* as well as in *Màrt
Earraich*, and that in the islands meal made with the Quern
(Bràthuin), and from brown oats, which are the kind of oats
most common in these islands, is stronger and more nourishing
food than common meal.   The merits of goat's milk are well
known.   This description of the best kind of deer-hound is
striking, and was taken down from a reciter in Skye.

II.—THE TWO HORSES.   Two horses were standing side by
side, ready yoked and ready to commence ploughing, when the
youngest, who was but newly broken, and a stranger to field
work, said, "We will plough this ridge and then that other
ridge and after that the next one, and once we have commenced
we will do every ridge in sight, and once we have fairly
commenced we will not be long in doing the whole field."   The
old horse, who had experience of the work, said, "We will
plough this furrow itself first."

III.—THE TWO DOGS.   There was a big, sleek, honest-
looking dog, and a little yelping cur of "low degree" was
always annoying him, and barking at him.   One day he caught

the little cur, and gave him a squeeze and sent it off yelping.
When the cur recovered itself it said, "I will not hurt you or
touch you, but I will raise an ill report *(droch-alla)* about you."
In pursuance of his threat the cur went among his acquaint-
ances, and such as he himself was.   There are many dogs to be
found in every town.

> " Both mongrel puppy whelp and hound
>   And curs of low degree."

and to such the cur related how the big dog for all his smooth
appearance and apparent good nature was in reality a cruel,
deceitful dog and under all his apparent or seeming good
manners, he was ready to fall upon those weaker than himself,
whether they gave him cause or not, and if he could do it
without being observed give them a bad shaking.   He was a
dangerous dog and ought to be watched and no wise dog should
put himself in his way.

This calumny made its way, found many believers and at
last produced its natural fruit.   The big honest dog found his
company avoided and every body looking upon him with
suspicion.

At first the depression, and gloom which haunted him disappeared under a hearty run, and the patting of its master, but
it preyed so much on him that he came to avoid society, and
to be apparently indifferent to any company,   This happens in
the experiences of life, and that causeless and evil reports are
most dangerous in their consequences,   Some time afterwards
the cur was similarly dealt with by another cur, who like himself had not very high principles.

THE CAT AND THE MOUSE.

A Gaelic Nursery Rhyme.

———

The Mouse said from her hiding place,
  "What are you about, Grey Cat?"
"Friendship, fellowship and love:
  You may come out!"
"Well I know the hooked claw
  That is fastened in the sole of your feet
You killed my sister yesterday,
  And with difficulty I myself escaped,
You thieving cat, son of the grim grey one,
  Where were you yesterday when from home?"
"I went away on my left hand
  To hunt for mince-meat in an evil hour;
I was noticed by the goodman of the house,
  My eye being shut and my cheek full;
He tightened my throat very hard,
  And called out to bring him the cheese-knife,
He cut off one of my ears
  And the red root of the ear to the bone."

Thuirt an Luchag, 's i 's an fhròig,
  "'Dé th' air t' aire, a Chait Ghlais?"
"Càirdeas 's comunn 's gaol:
  Feudaidh tusa tighinn a mach."
"Is eòlach mi air an dubhan chrom
  'Tha 'n sàs ann am bonn do chas!
Mharbh thu mo phiuthar an dé,
  'S ann air éiginn 'fhuair mi-fhéin as.
A chaoitein, mhic Ghrìmeich Ghlais,

C' àit an robh thu 'n raoir air chuairt?"
"Dh' fhalbh mi air mo làimh-chlì
   'Shealg nan ìsbean 's an droch uair;
Mhothaich fear-an-tighe dhomh,
   Mo shùll druidte 's mo phluic làn;
Theannaich e m' amhach gu cruaidh,
   'S ghlaodh e nuas air corc a' chàis,
Thug e dhiom-sa an leth-chluas
   'S am faillein ruadh gu ruig an cnàimh."

NOTE.

The foregoing rhyme is here given as being a more complete version than that to be found in vol. II. p. 389 (new edition p. 404) of "Popular Tales of the West Highlands" by the late J. F. Campbell, of Islay.

GAMES.

BOY'S GAMES.

In the Highlands of Scotland, as in every other place where there are children, youthful plays and amusements had their sway, and it is worthy of attention how these amusements were eminently calculated to develop and strengthen mind and muscular strength in the young. The various amusements of Riddles, and the many forms of indoor or house games are too numerous to describe, and in many instances not worth while dwelling upon. These games particularly called out the power of close attention and of ready speech, and were as often played out of doors as indoors, according to weather.

I.

WRESTLING MATCHES.

When the youth of a village met at a *cèilidh*, or indoor gathering, and a wrestling match was resolved upon, one of them was appointed a king or master of the ceremonies, and the company was bound to be obedient to him in everything. In the following game a stout and likely lad was fixed upon to come in, in the character of a "Desert Glede" (*Croman Fàsaich*). When he came in, the following speech occurred : addressing the king, he said :—

Croman.

"Leigeadh da, leigeadh da, Dia,"

Righ.

"Co as a thàinig thu, a Chromain Fhàsaich, no 'de an dràsda thug so thu ?"

Croman.

"Thàinig mi a m' fhonn 's a m' fhearann, 's a m' fhàsach fhéin."

Righ.

"'Dé chuir fearann 's fonn 's fàsach agadsa 's mise gun fhonn gun fhearann gun fhàsach."?

Croman.

"Mo chruas, 's mo luathas, 's mo làidireachd fhéin."

Righ.

"Tha òganach geur donn agamsa a leagadh tu, 's a bhreab-adh tu, 's a bheireadh sia deug dh' iallan do dhroma asad, agus iall g'ad cheangal; 's a mhi-mhodhaicheadh do bhean ann an clais na h-inne 's tu fhéin ceangailte."

Croman.

"Cuir a mach so e ma ta."

—————

Kite, or Glede.

"Permit, permit, O Deity."

King.

"Where have you come from, Kite of the Desert, and what has now brought you here?"

Kite.

"I come from my own land and soil and desert."

King.

"How have you land and soil and desert, when I have neither land nor soil nor desert?"

Kite.

"My own hardiness and swiftness and strength."

King.

"I have a smart brown-haired youth, who can throw you down, and kick you, and take sixteen thongs out of your back, and a thong to tie you with, and who can throw your wife into the byre gutter while you yourself are tied."

Kite.

"Send him out here then"

The wrestling then began, and the one who proved victor

I

became " Desert Glede " for the next encounter, until the whole were run over.

The words were sometimes used in the following form :—

Righ.—" Dida-a-didacha-dìsa, a Chromain Fhàsaich, co as dràsda a choisich thu ?"

Croman.—" Feuch 'bheil giomanach donn agad a chumas rium."

Righ —" Tha agamsa giomanach donn a chumas riut 's a dheanadh loth pheallagach dhiot aig dorus an tighe, etc."

————

King.—" Deeda-a-deedacha-deesa, Desert Glede, whence have you walked from now ?"

Kite.—" Try whether you have a brown-haired youth to match me."

King.—" I have a brown-haired youth that will match you and make a matted colt of you at the door of the house, etc."

————

Another game popular on these occasions was one of forfeits, known as the "Parson's mare has gone amissing," *(Làir a' pharsonaich air chall).* Every boy and girl in the company has a false name, given for the occasion, such as " Old Cow's Tail " *(Earball Seana Mhairt)*; " Rooster on the House-top " *(Coileach air Tigh),* etc. The king, or overseer, commencing the game says,

" The parson's mare has gone amissing,
And it is a great shame that it should be so ;
Try who stole her."

Làir a' pharsonaich air chall,
'S mòr an nàire dh' i bhi ann ;
Feuch cò ghoid i.

Looking round the circle, he fixes upon some one, and mentions him by the assumed name. He fixes, for instance, on the one to whom the name of "Old Cow's Tail" was given, and the person mentioned or denoted was bound at once to answer, saying

> " It 's a lie from you "
>
> ('S breugach dhuit e)

to which the answer is,

> " Who then is it ?"
>
> (Feuch cò eile e ?).

The person accused at once passes it on by mentioning some one else, such as the " Rooster on the House top," and the same query and answer, " Who then is it ?", etc., is passed on. The first one who fails in giving a ready reply has to submit to give a forfeit which the ruler keeps in security till all have been exacted ; then some one bends down and rests his head upon the king's knee, when the forfeits are held upon his head and he is made to award the punishment of redeeming them. He does not see whose forfeit it is, and the penalty imposed is sometimes very ludicrous and impossible. One, for instance, has to sit on the fire till his stomach boils (*Suidhe air an teine gus am bi a ghoile air ghoil)* ; another is to go out to the hillock in front of the village and bawl out three times,

> " This is the one who did the mischief
>
> And who will do it to-night yet."

> ('S mise an duine a rinn an t-olc
>
> 'S ni mi 'n nochd fhathast e).

This game requires great readiness and retentiveness of mind. The attention being kept continually on the strain in case one's own assumed name be called out, and a readiness to pass the accusation on to another.

The game of " Hide and Seek " was practised in the Highlands in many forms. Probably the earliest and simplest is that of young children playing round their mother, while she was engaged in baking bread. It was the custom in olden times to gather the meal or remains of dough left over after the oatcakes of bread were made, and duly work it into a cake by itself, called the *Bonnach Beag,* or "Little Cake," also known as *Siantachan a' Chlàir,* "The Charmer of the Board," which was supposed to be of mysterious value in keeping want away from the house. This little cake was given to the children, and when butter was ready or accessible, was thickly covered and given to the little fry, making a very welcome and grateful treat. Sometimes when the butter was very thickly spread, and perhaps with the thumb as the readiest and most convenient substitute for a knife, the housewife said, "Here take that; it is better than a hoard of cloth" (Gabh sin; 's fhearr e na mìr liath 'an clùd). Hence the expression that was used to denote that the preparations were not quite over :

"Cha 'n 'eil am bonnach beag bruich fhathast."

(The little cake is not ready yet).

Not infrequently the little things hid their heads under their mother's apron, thinking, like the ostrich of the desert that if their heads were hidden, none of the rest of them would be seen. When children played the game in the open air, the stackyard was commonly resorted to, and the one who was fixed upon as the Blind Man, while the rest were hiding themselves had to call out three times,

"Opera-opera-bo-baideag"

adding at the third time,

"Dalladh agus bodharadh agus dìth na dà chluais air an fhear nach cuala sud."

(Blindness and deafness and the loss of both ears be the lot of the one who will not hear that).

The Blind-man then caught hold of one of the stacks, and went round, guided by his hands, giving occasional kicks in case any one should be hiding himself near the ground.

APPENDIX.

I.—FINLAY GUIVNAC.

(Page 44).

Guibhnich, or *Duimhnich*, were the Campbells.   In a song in dispraise of the clan occurs,

> "Bheir mi 'n sgrìob so air na Guibhnich
> Air son cuimhneachadh o nuadh.
>
> (I will make this line on the Campbell clan,
> To remind them anew);

and in another similar song,

> "Sgrìos a' chorrain air a' choinnlein
> Air na bheil beò do na Guibhnich."
>
> (The destruction of the reaping-hook
>   on a grain of corn
> On the living race of the Campbell clan).

In Stewart's Collection, p. 320, is found,

> "Dean mo ghearan gu cuimhneach
> Ris na Duimhnidh ghlan uasal."
>
> (Be mindful to lay my complaint
> Before the pure-minded noble Campbells).

II.—PORT-NAN-LONG.

(Page 52).

Port-nan-long is said to have got its name from the following circumstance :—About the year 500 A.D., the few inhabitants then living in Tiree were in the township and neighbourhood of Sorabi, where there was a chapel, and which lies on the south-east side of the island, and is separated by the stream of the same name running past the burying-ground into the bay, from the township of Balinoe *(Baile-nodha)*. The island having been previously desolated by pirates and cattle-raiders, and a rumour being heard at this time that a band of these had again returned among the islands to renew their depredations, a watch was kept, and the factor of the community, who appears to have been their only protector and counsellor, went daily to look seawards for the appearance of the enemy, lest the small and feeble band might be surprised before they could make their escape or reach a hiding-place. One day then he saw ships coming from the south-east, and he went in and sent word to his neighbours. When he looked again, the ships were nearer and were a large fleet. The next look he gave he saw that they were close at hand, near the land. He then called the people round him, and told them how he could see that their enemies, who were near, were too powerful to be resisted; that as he himself and those with him were defenceless, and unable to escape, their only hope of deliverance from their terrible danger was in the power of Almighty God, whose aid he would ask, and kneeling on the ground with his friends and neighbours around him, he said, "O Lord, as all power is in thy hand, help us against these enemies who are coming on us (to destroy us)"; *(A Thighearna, o'n a's ann ad làimh a tha gach cumhachd, cuidich leinn o na naimhdean sin a tha 'tighinn oirnn!)*. He had scarcely uttered the last word when a violent storm came from the south-east, and the ships of the enemy came ashore, one heaped above another *(air muin a' chéile)*. Sixteen of them were completely destroyed. One person even was not left to tell their fate; and from that time the place has been called *Port-nan-long*, (the Creek of Boats).

III.—A TRADITION OF MORAR.

MAC VIC AILEIN OF MORAR *(Mòr-thìr)* was out in a shealing
with his men, on a summer morning, and saw a young woman
following cows, with her petticoats gathered to keep them dry,
as the dew was heavy on the ground *(a còtaichean truiste, le
truimead an driùchd, g' an cumail tioram)*. He said, "Would
not that be a handsome young woman if her two legs were not
so slender *(mur biodh caoilead a dà choise)*." She answered in
his hearing, "Often a slender-shanked cow has a large udder[1]
(is minig a bha ùth mhòr aig bò chaol-chasach)." He asked her
to be brought where he was ; she was his own dairymaid. She
went away to Ireland, and named her son Murdoch after his
foster-father *(oide)*, whom she afterwards married. He was
known as Little Murdoch MacRonald *(Murcha beag Mac
Raonuill)*. As he grew older his mother would be telling him
about a brother he had in Alban *(an Albainn)* who was a
strong and powerful man, and the lad, being a good wrestler,
thought he would like to go and see him, to try a bout of
wrestling *(car-gleachd)* with him, to find which of them was the

---

1. In the oldest known version of the Exile of the Son of Usnech
(preserved in the 12th century MS., the Book of Leinster) when Noisi
sees Deirdre for the first time, he exclaims, ' 'Tis a fair heifer passing
by me.' She answers, ' Where the bulls are there must needs be fine
heifers.' This is one of the passages relied upon by Prof. Zimmer in
support of his contention that old Irish literature is so extremely
'naturalistic' in its treatment of sexual matters that we must needs
suppose the Aryan Celts were polluted by a rude and more archaic
population. I confess I see nothing in either the earlier or the present
passage but the simplicity of a race living, 2000 years ago, as it
still in part does, very close to nature, and accustomed to frank
speaking about natural matters. The whole of this tradition is simply
the fitting into a local frame of incidents which are commonplaces in
the folk-tales.—A. N.

strongest man, and watched for an opportunity to get to Alban. As there was frequent communication then between Ireland and the Western Highlands he had not long to wait till he saw a boat in which it was likely he would be taken. He went to the harbour and on reaching the boat, without knowing that it belonged to his brother, asked the first person he met, who was *Mac vic Ailein* himself, if he would get ferried across to Scotland *(dh' iarr e'n t-aiseag)*. *Mac vic Ailein* said that he would take him with them. When they went away the day became stormy *(shéid an latha)*, and no one who went to steer but was lifted from the helm,[2] *Mac vic Ailein* being thrown aside as well as the others. When *Murcha beag Mac Raonuill* saw that the strongest man among them could not stand at the helm, he asked to be allowed to try it. "You would get that," *Mac vic Ailein* said, "if you were like a man who was able to do it, but when it is beyond our strength *('nuair a dh' fhairtlich i oirnn fhéin)*, you need not make the attempt." "At anyrate," he said "I will give it a trial": and it did not make him alter his position *(cha do chuir i thar a bhuinn e)* till they reached land. As he was the best seaman *Mac vic Ailein* would not part with him. He took him to his house and entertained him as a guest. They entered into conversation and began to give news to each other *(chaidh iad gu seanachas agus gu naigheachdan)* till little Murdoch told him he was his brother and that it was for the express purpose *(a dh' aon obair)* of seeing him he had come from Ireland, and that he would not return till they tried a bout of wrestling, since *Mac vic Ailein* was so renowned for his prowess, and he would find out what strength he possessed before he left. The heroes rose and began to wrestle, but in a short time *Mac vic Ailein* was thrown *(Dh' éirich na suinn, ach ann an tiota bha Mac 'ic Ailein 's a*

---

2. The helm was worked by being caught by the shoulders of the steersman as it worked backwards and forwards *('g a cheapadh le 'shlinneanan a null 's a nall)*

dhruim ri talamh). " I am pleased to have taken the trouble of coming from Ireland *(toilichte as mo shaothair),*" Murdoch said. Next day at dinner they had beef on the table, and little Murdoch said, " Let us try which of us can break the shank bone[3] *(a' chama-dhubh)* with the hand closed." "I am willing," *Mac vic Ailein* said. " Well, try it, then," Murdoch said. *Mac vic Ailein* tried as hard as his strength would permit, and it defied him *(dh' fhairtlich i air).* Murdoch broke it at the first blow. *Mac vic Ailein* then said, " You will not return to Ireland any more ; you will stay with me, and we will divide the estate between us." Murdoch replied, " I am well to do as it is *(glé mhath dheth mar thà),* my mother and stepfather have sufficient worldly means *(gu leòir de 'n t-saoghal),* and I will not stay away from them though you were to give me the whole estate," and wishing *Mac vic Ailein* enjoyment and prosperity, he bade him farewell and returned to Ireland, and friendly communication was kept up between them ever afterwards during their lives.

---

3. *A' chama-dhubh,* the bone of the animal between the knee and shoulder-point *(na bha de 'n chnàimh eadar an glùn agus an t-alt-lùthainn).*

,ℼ,p 52

IV.—CORRESPONDENCE BETWEEN J. F. CAMPBELL
OF ISLAY AND J. G. CAMPBELL.

Among the treasures regarding folk-lore that I have been able to collect are a few letters of the late J. F. Campbell of Islay to the Rev. J. G. Campbell, late Minister of Tiree. They deal with various questions and traditions.

Inter alia is a discussion concerning the word sàil *versus* sìol Dhiarmaid. I give the letters as written.

A. CAMPBELL.

SÀIL OR SÌOL DHIARMAID.

The late Campbell of Islay to the late J. G. Campbell.

TRAVELLERS' CLUB,
Feb. 27, 1871.

MY DEAR SIR,

I'll get you the books you name and send them soon. With regard to sàil there was once an actor who amused an audience by putting his head under his cloak and squealing like a pig. A countryman rose and said that he would squeal better next day. So a match was made and tried. The audience applauded the actor and hissed the countryman. But he produced a pig from under his cloak. I know what the man meant who signed Sàil Dhiarmaid. The man who spoke no other language pointed to the place in his foot which he meant by Sàil, so I learned the lesson, and anybody who will try may learn a good deal about Gaelic in the same fashion.

If a man starts with the conviction that knowledge is to the unknown as a drop in the ocean—he will get on.

I have MacNicol, and know his remark about Ossian's leg.

I have now got the only copy that ever was written, so far as I know, and I shall be glad to get more. But we must all take what we can get. As far as fixing the king or the country and the date, that is perfectly hopeless. I have about 16 versions of one story in

Gaelic, and no two have the same name.' I suppose that there must be sixty versions of it known in other languages, and no two are alike. The oldest I know is scattered in ejaculations and separate lines through the Rigveda Sanhitâ, which is a collection of hymns in Sansarit, and the oldest things known. St. George and the Dragon is a form of the story. Perseus and Andromeda is another. In Gaelic it is generally *Mac an Iasgair*, or *Iain Mac* somebody, or *Fionn Mac a' Bhradain,* a something to do with a mermaid or a dragon, the herding of cows and the slaying of giants. The stories to which I referred were told me by John Ardfenaig as facts (the Duke of Argyll's factor in the Ross of Mull). A man built a boat. Another, to spite him, said that the death of a man was in that boat—no one would go to sea in it, and at last the boat was sold by the builder to an unbeliever in ghosts and dreams. The other was how the turnips were protected in Tiree. If you know these you have got far, but if not you have a good deal to learn in Tiree.

I wish you success anyhow,

Yours truly,

J. F. CAMPBELL.

NIDDRY LODGE, KENSINGTON,
March 28, 1871.

MY DEAR SIR,

I have been too busy about festivities and work to be able to get the book which I promised to seek for you. I got your letter of the 20th, yesterday, and I am much obliged by your promise to put some one to write for me. If he writes from dictation will you kindly *beg him to follow the words spoken* without regard to his own opinion, or to what they ought to be. I speak English, but when I come to read Chaucer I find words that I am not used to. So it is when men who speak Gaelic begin to write old stories. Our argument is an illustration. You speak Gaelic and you believe that Sàil means heel and nothing else. You told me that Sàil Dhiarmaid ought to be Slol.

Now I speak Gaelic, but I profess to be a scholar, not a teacher. I happen to know that the man who signed Sàil Dhiarmaid, which was printed *Sàil* did'nt mean *Slol*. I have the following quotation,—

"Eisdibh beag ma's àill leibh laoidh

* * * * * * *

Chaidh am bior nimh' bu mhòr cràdh
An Sàil an laoich nach tlàth 's an trod—
'S e ri sior chall na fala
Le lot a' bhior air a bhonn."

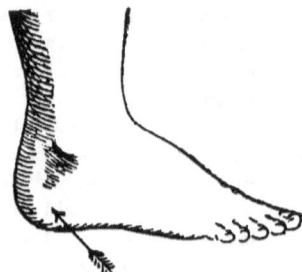

In this old lay as sung in the outer isles these would mean the spot which an old Mull man pointed to as sàil.*

If you are sceptical I hold to my creed of the people. But creed or no creed I want to get the tradition as it exists and I would not give a snuff for "cooked" tradition.

* This discussion is doubtless concerning the spot where tradition says the bristle of the boar wounded Diarmaid when he measured the length of the dead beast.—A C.

Tuesday, Oct. 10, 1871.
CONAN HOUSE, DINGWALL.

MY DEAR SIR,

I promised yesterday at Portree to send you my version of the fairy song, and asked you to return yours. You must remember that I never tried to write it from Gaelic, and that I never tried to write it from rapid dictation till last month. Correct my spelling, but mind that I took the *sounds* from ear, so preserve all that you can without reference to dictionary words. Don't be hard upon a clansman who is doing his best.

Believe me,
Yours very truly,
J. F. CAMPBELL.

From John Cameron, a man about 60, who lives in the south end of Barra, about three miles from Castlebay. He can sing and recite, 1.—The Maiden (written by J. F. C.); 2.—The Death of Diarmaid; 3.—The Death of Osgar; 4.—The Battle of Manus (written by J. F. C.); 5.—The story of the Death of Garry; 6.—The Black Dog; 7.— The story of ditto. 8.—The Smithy and story; 9.—The *Muireartach*; 10.—Dàn an Deirg; 11.—The Fairy Song (as written here by J. F. C.); 12.—How Coireal was slain; 13.—Fionn's questions; 14.—A small story written; and sundry other songs, lays, and stories, which he will get written if I wish it. This is one of about a dozen of men whom I have met of late who can sing and recite Ossianic ballads, of which some are not in any book or old manuscript that I know. I have another version of this song, written about ten years ago—by MacLean,* I think. See Vol. IV. Popular Tales, Lists somewhere. It is now in London.

* Hector MacLean, Ballygrant, Islay: now dead.—A. C.

THE FAIRY SONG.

The tune is very wild and like a pibroch. I could not learn it in the time.

Wants IV. 2

FFLox
8,
Super

This is the story as told in Gaelic.

There was a time, at first, when before children were christened they used to be taken by the fairies. A child was born and it was in a woman's lap. A fairy came to the *Bean-ghlùn* and she said to the midwife, "*'S trom do leanabh.*" "*'S trom gach torrach,*" said the other. "*'S aotrom do leanabh,*" said the fairy. "*'S aotrom gach soghalach,*" said the midwife, *'S glas do leanabh,*" said the fairy. "*'S glas am fiar 's fàsaidh e,*" said the other; and so she came day by day with words and with singing of verses to try if she could "word" him away with her—"*am briatharachadh i leatha è.*" But the mother always had her answer ready. There was a lad recovering from a fever in the house and he heard all these words, and learned them, and he put the song together afterwards: after the child was christened the fairy came back no more.

This is the song. I have tried to divide the words so as to represent the rhythm of the tune, but I am not sure that I have succeeded.—J. F. C.

I have given a rough copy to Miss MacLeod of MacLeod at Dunvegan, and I should like to have *this* or *a copy* back if it is not troublesome. My first manuscript is not easy to read, and I have worked this from it.

Fairy :—"'S e mo leanabh mìleanach
      Seachd Maileanach
      Seachd Dhuanach,
      Gual na lag; 's lag na luineach
      Nach d' fhàs "nacach."

[Reciter don't understand gnathach, common.]

Mother :—Se mo leanabh ruiteach (colour ruddy)
　　　　Reamhar molteach
　　　　Miuthear mo luachair
　　　　Ohog ri mnathan
　　　　M' eòin 'us m' uighean
　　　　On thug thu muine leat
　　　　'Us maire leat
　　　　'Us mo chrodh lùigh
　　　　'Us mo lochraidh leat.

Mother :—Bha thu fo 'm chrios an uire
　　　　'S tha thu 'm bliadhna
　　　　Gu cruinn buanach
　　　　Air mo guailain
　　　　Feadh a bhaile.

Fairy :—Thug go gu gŏrach (fat, Reciter)
　　　　Mnath 'n òg a bhaile
　　× Lan *shaochail** uimach
　　　　Thug go gu gŏrach
　　　　Le 'n ciabhan dhonna
　　　　Le 'n ciabhan troma

[He said at first somewhere, "Le 'n ciochan corrach " ? place.]

　　　　Thug go gu gŏrach
　　　　'S le 'n suilean donna

Mother :—Se sin Leoid
　　　　Na lorg 's na luireach
　　　　Se Lochlan bu duchas dhuit
　　　　O fire fire nì mi uimad
　　　　Cireadh do chinn
　　　　Ni mi uimad.

Fairy :—Fire fire nì mi uimad
　　　　Cha tu an uan beag

× ——→

Ni mi uimad
Crodh 'us caorich
Ni mi uimad.

Mother :—Fire fire ni mi uimad
Breachan chaola
Ni mi uimad
Fire fire ni mi uimad
A bhog mhiladh (? fileadh. Oh soft soldier,
soft mine own)
O bhòg 's leam thu
O bhog mhìlidh bhog
Mo bhrù a rug
O bhog mhilidh bhog
Mo chioch a thug
O bhog mhilidh bhog
Mo gluin a thog
O bhog mhilidh
Bho 's leam thu.

Fairy :—B' fheàrr leam gu faic mi do bhuaille
Gu àrd àrd an iomal sleibhe
Còta geal cateanach† uaine
Mu do ghuailain ghil 'us léine.

Nurse :—B' fhearr leam gu faichean do sheisearach
Fir na deance (?) a cuit shìl
Gu rò do cheol air feadh do thalla (land or
hall)
Leann bhi ga gabhail le fìon
Bhog mhìlidh bhog
'S leam thu.

---

* Suobhcail or saobh chiall.
† Hairy, rough, shaggy.

And so she says a verse each day, and if that would not do, she came the next and made another, and the little lad made out the song which he sat and heard. When the child was baptized she went away and never came back again.

N.B.—I have set the verses to each character as best I could, not knowing much about it except the last two, these the reciter placed.

NOTE.

The Fairy Song in the MS. is most difficult to read. It was written phonetically, and is now in some places indistinct. The following transliteration and translation by Mr. Duncan Mac Isaac, of Oban, show a probable reading, and this may be enough, in view of the spell-words of the fairy, whose mystic diction appears to have been of a conservative quality, and to have affected the responses of the infant's mother.—[A. C.]

  Fairy—'S e mo leanabh mì-loinneach
    Seac maoileanach
    Seac ghuanach,
    Guailne lag, 's lag 'n a lùireach
    Nach d' ùisinnicheadh.

  Mother :—'S e mo leanabh ruiteach
    Reamhar moltach
    M' iubhar mo luachair
    A thog ri mnathan
    M' eòin is m' uighean
    O 'n thug thu m' ùine leat
    Is m' aire leat
    Is mo chrodh-laoigh
    Is mo laochraidh leat.

Mother :—Bha thu fo 'm chrios an uiridh
       'S tha thu 'm bliadhna
       Gu cruinn buanach
       Air mo ghualainn
       Feadh a' bhaile.

Fairy :—Thuth gò gugurach
       Mnathan òg a' bhaile
       Làn shòghail uidheamach
       Thuth gò gugurach
       Le 'n ciabhan donna
       Le 'n ciabhan troma
       Thug go gugurach
       Le 'n ciochan corrach
       'S le 'n sùilean donna.

Mother :—'S e sin Leòid
       'N a lorg 's 'n a lùireach
       'S Lochlann bu dùthchas dhuit
       O fire fire nì mi umad
       Cìreadh do chinn
       Nì mi umad.

Fairy :—Fire fire nì mi umad
       Cha tu an t-uan beag
       Nì mi umad.
       Crodh is caoraich
       Nì mi umad.

Mother :—Fire fire nì mi umad
       Breacain chaola
       Nì mi umad
       Fire fire uì mi umad
       A bhog mhìlidh
       . O bhog 's leam thu

O bhog mhìlidh bhog
Mo bhrù a rug
O bhog mhìlidh bhog
Mo chloch a thug
O bhog mhìlidh bhog
Mo ghlùin a thog
O bhog mhìlidh
Bho 's leam thu.

Fairy :—B' fheàrr leam gu faic mi do bhuaile
Gu àrd àrd 'an iomall sléibhe
Còta geal caiteineach uaine
Mu do ghualainn ghil is léine.

Mother :—B' fheàrr leam gu faicinn do sheisreach
Fir na deannaige a' cur sìl
Gu robh do cheòl air feadh do thalla
Leann 'bhi 'g a ghabhail le fìon
Bhog mhìlidh bhog
'S leam thu.

Fairy :—He is my ungraceful child,
Withered, bald, and light-headed,
Weak-shouldered, and weak in his equipments,
That have not been put to use.

Mother :—He is my ruddy child, plump and praiseworthy ;
My yew-tree, my rush, raised to women ;
My bird and my eggs, since thou hast taken my
time with thee,
My watchful care, my calved-cows, and my heroes
with thee ;
Last year thou wast under my girdle,
Thou art this year neatly gathered
Continually upon my shoulder
Through the town.

Fairy :—Hooh go googurach,
      Young women of the town, fond of delicacies and
         dresses,
      Hooh go googurach,
      With their brown ringlets, with their heavy tresses,
      With their abrupt breasts, with their brown eyes.

Mother :—That is a Mac Leod by heredity
      In his coat of mail ;
      Thy nativity is Scandinavian ;
      O pother, pother, the combing of thy head,
      I'll do that about thee.

Fairy :—Pother, pother, I'll do about thee ;
      Thou art not the little lamb
      I'll make about thee,
      Cattle and sheep I'll make about thee.

Mother :—Pother, pother, I'll do about thee,
      Narrow plaids I'll make about thee,
      O pother I'll make about thee, thou soft warrior,
      O tender one, thou art mine, thou soft soldier,
      The fruit of my womb, thou soft, tender warrior,
      My breast that took, thou soft champion,
      Reared upon my knees, thou tender champion,
      Since thou art mine.

Fairy :—I'd prefer to see thy cattle-fold
      High, high on the shoulder of the mountain,
      A white coat, ruffled green,
      About thy white shoulders, and a shirt.

Mother :—I'd prefer to see thy team of horses,
      And the men of the handfuls sowing seed,
      And that thy music would be through thy hall
      Accompanied by ale and wine ;
      Thou tender champion,
      Thou art mine.

The late Campbell of Islay in the following letter, extracts of which will be given, alludes to Mr. Campbell's intention of publishing at no distant date.

NIDDRY LODGE, Jan., 16, 1871.

I thank you for your letter of the 10th which reached me on Saturday, on my return to Tiree.

I shall be very glad to assist a namesake and a Highland minister who is engaged in literary work, in which I take a special interest myself. I now repeat my message, and ask you to place my name on the list of subscribers, if you have one. I shall be very glad to read your book. I am not publishing more Gaelic tales, but I am collecting, and I may some day publish a selection or an abstract or something from a great mass which I have got together. If you have anything to spare from your gatherings perhaps the best plan would be to employ some good scribe, etc. etc. etc. If you have any intention of publishing I beg that you will not think of sending me your gatherings. But anything sent will be carefully preserved.

Superstitions are very interesting, but I should fear that the people will not confide their superstitions to the minister. Amongst other matters which are noteworthy are superstitious practices about fowls.

These prevail in Scotland, and are identical with sacrifices by the blacks amongst whom Speke and Grant travelled—so Grant told me. Anything to do with serpents has special interest because of the extent of ancient serpent worship, for which see Ferguson's great book on Tree and Serpent Worship in India and elsewhere. The connection between tree and well worship in India and in Scotland generally, and generally in the old world, is well worth investigation ; also anything that is like the Vedic forms of religion, at which you can get by reading Wilson's Translation of the Rigveda Sanhitâ, and the works of Max Muller. Anything belonging specially to the sea is interesting. The Aryans are supposed to have been natives of Central Asia, to whom the sea must have been a great mystery.

Now it is a fact that all the Aryan nations have curious beliefs and ceremonies and practices about going to sea, *e.g.*—you must not whistle at sea ; you must not name a mouse *Luds* in Argyll but *Biast tighe* ; you must not say the shore names for *fine* or *low* when at sea, but use sea terms ; all that is curious and very hard to get at. Even to me they will not confess their creed in the supernatural. I have a great lot of stuff that might be useful to you, and I shall be glad to serve you, because there is a certain narrow-minded spirit abroad to which reference is made in the paper which I send herewith. It is highly probable that I may be out in the west in spring or summer.

Yours very truly,

J. F. CAMPBELL.

The following letter refers to the longest and most complex tale orally preserved in the Highlands, 'The Leeching of Kian's Leg.' The version which Islay mentions is still unprinted. It is preserved with a portion of his MSS. in the Advocate's Library at Edinburgh, and a summary of its contents has been published by me in *Folk-Lore*, Vol. I., p. 369. Mr. Campbell's fragmentary version was printed and translated by him, 'Transactions of the Gaelic Society of Inverness, 1888.' Another fragmentary version, collected by the Rev. D. MacInnes, will be found in Vol. II. of this series. The oldest known MS. version, alluded to in this letter, has been edited and translated by Mr. Standish Hayes O'Grady in *Silva Gadelica*, from a 15th century MS. A re-telling of the story, based upon all the versions, will be found in Mr. Jacob's *More Celtic Fairy Tales.*—A. N.

May, 4, 71. NIDDRY LODGE,
KENSINGTON.

MY DEAR SIR,
I sent you a *Times* review of Clerk's Ossian the other day to amuse you ; also a paper with an account of fighting in Paris, where I was at Easter.

I got your letter and parcel of May 1, last night, and I have just read the story. It is extremely well written, and the language is vernacular and perfectly genuine : as I have now got 20 volumes, and half another, I am able to judge. Yours is a version of the story of which I sent you the abstract. If ever I publish the story I see that I must fuse versions, and select from the majority of various readings, under the name of "The Leching of Khene is legg." The story is mentioned in the Catalogue of the Earl of Kildare's library amongst the Irish Books, A.D. 1526 (Harleian MSS., 3756, Brit. Museum). I gave this information to Kildare, who has been hunting high and low to find out what was meant, they could not tell him in Ireland. I met him at Lorne's marriage and lent him my copy, 142 pages from oral recitation. Now you send me 19 more pages, and 3 of another version, 22. Between us we have already recovered something of a story 345 years old at least.

Therefore Tradition is respectable ; a comparison of versions gives a fair measure of the power of popular memory, so that written Gaelic folk-lore is a kind of measure for other and older written traditions. But as all that is old in history was tradition at first, the study is worth trouble as I judge. The more we can get written the better pleased I shall be. I am exceedingly obliged to you, and hope to thank you in person some of these days.

I am,

Yours truly,

J. F. CAMPBELL.

Archibald Sinclair Printer Celtic Press, 10 Bothwell Street, Glasgow.

www.ingramcontent.com/pod-product-compliance
Lightning Source LLC
Chambersburg PA
CBHW020227030726
47497CB00009B/2990